The task of moving from t... faithful exposition is challeng... aims to help the Bible teacher t... and prepare to convey its signi... In this way these volumes oft... weightier technical commentaries. It is li... ...ng the guidance of an experienced coach in the wonderful work of rightly handling the word of truth.

John Woodhouse
Principal,
Moore College,
Sydney, Australia

North India desperately needs men and women who will preach and teach the Bible faithfully and PT's Teaching series is of great value in encouraging them to do just that. They are just what we need. We have found the books of great help in English and eagerly anticipate the day when they will be available in Hindi also.

Isaac Shaw
Executive Director,
Delhi Bible Institute

TEACHING EPHESIANS

From text to message

SIMON AUSTEN

SERIES EDITORS: DAVID JACKMAN & ADRIAN REYNOLDS

PT RESOURCES

CHRISTIAN
FOCUS

Contents

SERIES PREFACE

There is no doubt that Ephesians is a key New Testament book, dealing as it does with the nature and life of the church. Containing some of the most well known Bible sections (saved by grace; marriage; the armour of God), Ephesians is much more than a treasury of Sunday school lessons. Here is a closely argued, warmly applied letter from the heart of the Apostle to the Gentiles, reflected in Simon's careful analysis for the Bible preacher or teacher. His love of the book and understanding of its relevance for today come through clearly in this important contribution to the Teaching the Bible series.

It is the eleventh volume in the series: as with all the others, it is focused on those who have the joyful but serious privilege of preaching and teaching God's Word. The first section contains some introductory material to get you into the text of Ephesians. This is followed by the 'meat' of the book, working systematically through the letter, suggesting possible preaching or teaching units, including sermon outlines and questions for Bible studies. These are not there to take the hard work out of preparation, but as a starting point to get you thinking about how to preach the material or prepare a study.

We continue to be encouraged at how the series is developing and, more importantly, how it is being received by those who really matter – men and women at the chalk face of Christian ministry, working hard at the Word of God, week in week out, to proclaim the unsearchable riches of Christ.

Our thanks go, as ever, to the team at Christian Focus for their committed partnership in this project.

David Jackman & Adrian Reynolds
Series Editors, London,
March 2012

AUTHOR'S PREFACE

One of the delights and challenges of teaching the Bible is that we never stop learning. Year in, year out we re-visit old haunts and seemingly familiar passages. Gradually the Word does its work in our lives, teaching, correcting, rebuking and encouraging. We realise that what we once thought or taught has not done justice to the text; that we have allowed our doctrinal presuppositions to triumph over our exegetical rigour; that we have naively assumed a book is finished and understood.

As we wrestle again and again with the text and prayerfully listen to the words we thought we knew so well, we emerge with greater clarity, greater humility and a greater passion for the things of God. It means that any book which has been written which attempts to explain a book of the Bible will take us only so far. It may give us some tools to dig deeper or confidence to wrestle with the text ourselves. It may point us in the right direction, but it can never be a substitute for our own reading, study and prayer. This book can, therefore, be no more than an imperfect tool that might help us to understand a little more clearly the perfect Word of God.

The power and significance of Ephesians has emerged for me from ministry in the local church. The necessity and relevance of its words have been made all the more tangible by seeing them worked out in the battles and blessings of local church ministry. I am grateful for the way in which the local church I am privileged to pastor has helped me to see why these words are so important; and for all those in other contexts who have invited me to preach from this letter: in other local churches, at church weekends away, on conferences and to student groups.

I am grateful, too, for all those who have assisted me in my writing and encouraged me in preaching: for Sam Parkinson, Adrian Reynolds and David Jackman in their editorial work and wise advice; for the Proclamation Trust in helping me to learn how to preach and for giving me opportunities to teach others; for Alasdair Paine, who shared a conference with me in Brazil during which I preached through the material in this book and gave careful advice along the way; above all, for my wonderful wife, Fiona, whose support and godliness have made Ephesians come alive in the home. I hope and pray that those who use this book may discover a renewed love for God and for the local church of which we are a part – for there we find the purposes of God for the world.

Simon Austen
Carlisle,
January 2012

How to Use this Book

This book is intended to give those who read it both an understanding of the book of Ephesians and also a hunger to study it and preach it. It may not have all the detail of a more academic commentary, but it seeks to interact with the text and enable those who use it to understand the letter in a way which will make sense to the everyday church member. Equally, it may be used as an aid to preparing Bible-studies and to that end each section provides some suggested questions for small groups alongside the suggested sermon headings for the preacher.

It is preferable, where possible, to study the letter and read the book before preparing any sermons or Bible studies. In that way we will have put ourselves in the place of the original hearers, listening to all the words together and making sense of the whole before we presume to preach or teach the part.

A note about sermon headings

Some preachers are particularly good at preparing memorable titles for sermons and sermon points, whether

by alliteration, association or acronym. Others may not
be able to do this so well but may be sufficiently gifted as
speakers for the points preached to be clearly and helpfully
presented without particularly memorable words.

Throughout the book I have given some suggestions
for sermon headings. Many of them are not particularly
catchy and I am not sure that it really matters. It depends,
in some ways, what our sermon headings are there to do.
The classic preaching model of 'state, explain, illustrate,
apply' may leave the preacher deciding to make his
heading from his point of application, thereby leaving
his hearers with the implications of the text in their
mind. Other preachers may use a heading to create
a space into which the passage speaks or indeed to deal
with the issues raised by the introduction, each of which
may be explained by the passage as it is expounded. Still
others may use handouts with headings or PowerPoint
presentations.

I am increasingly of the opinion that the Bible allows
for a variety of preaching 'styles' in which the personality of
the preacher and the context into which he preaches will
have an influence on how the sermon is structured. It is
striking that the New Testament does not provide us with
a particular model of preaching and that history is littered
with preachers who have been greatly used by God but do
not follow many rules when it comes to structure. Whatever
our style, we need to be prayerful, faithful and engaging.
The Word rightly preached is immensely powerful.

The sermon headings suggested can, therefore, be no
more than suggestions, helpful hints which may be adapted
and changed as we work with the text and prepare what we
have to preach.

A note about study groups

Many churches make use of small groups as a way of extending the teaching and pastoral ministry of a large congregation. They present a wonderful opportunity for Christian discipleship, evangelism and prayer and can be a tremendous example of the letter to the Ephesians in action. When done well, they can be extremely powerful forces for good in the local church.

Equally, perhaps, we should sound a note of caution. Unlike a sermon, the home group provides an opportunity to interact with the text and with one another, asking questions and sharing opinions. Positively, this allows home group members to deal with confusion and misunderstanding; to bring clarity from the fog which many of us have as we begin to study a new book or letter. Negatively, opinion-sharing can very easily place us in a position where we sit in judgement on the text rather than in submission to it. We can begin to decide what the text means, or what we would like it to mean without sufficient engagement with the words set before us.

For several years I have met monthly with my home group leaders. It has been a joy to look at the Bible together and a great privilege to grow together. We have sometimes used the imagery of swimming pool and a trampoline in our attempts to discern how to lead a Bible study. The trampoline allows us to bounce off the text and to return to the position with which we began; the swimming pool invites us to dive in, to immerse ourselves in the words and world of the Ephesians and to come out changed. It is the model of the swimming pool rather than the trampoline which must shape our teaching. We want to discover what God's Word meant in the first century so that we might know what it means in the twenty-first; we want to find out what God thinks rather than simply share what we think.

To that end, the most important part of leading a Bible study is thorough preparation. We need to be sure and certain of the text and how it fits into the wider letter if we are to handle it correctly. The questions we use may often give a direction and framework and help others to keep on track, but a confident leader may be able to ask their own appropriate questions as he or she works through the passage, even if those questions are not printed for the group. Equally, a few simple questions may open the door to others, or a summary of the study might be given out at the end or the beginning, with or without specific questions.

The aim in any study is for all who come to see for themselves what the Bible says, to discover what you have learnt in your preparation without them realising that they have done so. Such Bible studies in which all who participate share, but are also taught, rebuked, corrected and encouraged are rare, but perfectly possible with prayer and thorough preparation.

In many ways it can be harder to lead a study than to preach a passage but when done well it is possible that more will be learnt than in the context of regular preaching. Many people find it very helpful to have a home group series and a preaching series running in parallel, either using the same passage or combining passages in order to cover the whole book over a number of weeks.

Throughout this book I have provided suggested questions for each section, but in many ways personally written questions may enable the group leader to have more 'ownership' of the study. My own practice in preparing leaders is to work through the passage together, attempting to help them to understand what is going on by the questions I ask and then giving them some suggested questions at the end which they may use in their own groups, or adapt as required. My hope is that the suggested questions for study in this book might be used in a similar way.

Part I:
Introductory Material

I

GETTING OUR BEARINGS IN EPHESIANS

For most of us our experience of church is mixed. It is a great privilege and delight to be a part of God's new community, to know that sense of love and acceptance and forgiveness; it is wonderful when we experience that quality of life and love which can only come from the regenerating work of the Spirit. But churches can also be very difficult. People fall out with one another, cliques form, powerful individuals hold sway, pastors are criticised. There is all too often a large gulf between what we are in Christ and what we are in reality. The result of this is that as the main distinguishing mark of being a disciple is destroyed (love for one another) so the main responsibilities of the church are diminished (evangelism, prayer and nurture). It can be very difficult for us to be what we know we are in Christ.

Ephesians is a letter for the church, a timeless exposition about becoming what we are in Christ. It sets forth the objective reality for all who are recipients of God's unmerited love and who have been made alive in Christ; and then it tells us how we might become what we are. Reading and understanding Ephesians is like being taken through the theological equivalent of a photographer's dark room. In the days before digital photography the picture was captured at the moment the camera's shutter opened, permanently set into the film, yet it still had to be developed. There, in the dark room, the picture slowly emerged; that which had been taken became a permanent reality for all to see.

In the same way we have been made alive and raised with Christ. As a result we have every spiritual blessing in him. The picture has been taken; but now the film must be developed, so that we can become what we are. Ephesians takes us on that journey, explaining the nature of the picture that has been taken and how the photograph can be developed, so that those who are God's people might become what they have been made in Christ.

It is a letter which has generated rich emotion, being described as 'one of the most significant documents ever written.'[1] It has been said that it matches Romans 'as a candidate for exercising the most influence on Christian thought and spirituality.'[2] And yet it is a letter which many a preacher knows only in part. Its rich treasure for Christian thought and spirituality, and in particular its wonderfully developed doctrine of the church, remains relatively untapped. Our churches need to hear this letter. We need to be challenged about our consumerist and individualistic views of salvation and of our relationship to the people to which we have been called and of which we are a part. We need to think again about so-called homogenous churches

1   Peter O'Brien, *The Letter to the Ephesians* (Nottingham, UK: Apollos,1999) p. 1.
2   R.E. Brown, *An Introduction to the New Testament* (New York/London: Doubleday, 1997) p. 620.

and their potential misrepresentation of the gospel. And perhaps above all, we need to recapture the glorious reality of the local church as a beacon of the future and a picture of God's purposes in the world. The local church is not only the hope of the world; it also shows us where history is heading.

Ephesus in the New Testament

The city of Ephesus, although once a Greek colony, had become by Paul's day the capital city of Roman Proconsular Asia. Powerful and cosmopolitan, it hosted the headquarters of the cult of Artemis (Diana), whose temple, which was rebuilt after being destroyed in the 4th century B.C., was now considered to be one of the seven wonders of the ancient world. Sitting in the Amphitheatre today and looking out to the now silted-up port, it is easy to imagine the once-thriving commercial centre and the relatively low-profile arrival of Paul and his companions as he travelled from Corinth back towards Jerusalem on his second missionary journey expedition. His three-year ministry (52-55 A.D. cf. Acts 20:31) influenced all of Asia and left us with a treasure-trove of Biblical encouragement and warning.

Luke's account of Paul's Ephesian ministry dominates Acts 19 and 20. Initially Paul entered the synagogue, speaking boldly there for three months and arguing persuasively about the Kingdom of God. It is reasonable to assume that some of the Jews believed, not least because the letter he later wrote has so much to say about the relationship between Jew and Gentile but also because, when the opposition arose, Luke tells us that '*some* of them became obstinate and refused to believe', (italics mine).

Those who refused to respond 'publicly maligned the Way' (Acts 19:9). Others, presumably, didn't.

Those who had believed and were responding to the teaching moved with Paul to the lecture hall of Tyrannus, where he began a series of daily discussions which lasted for two years. As a result, 'All the Jews and Greeks who lived in the Province of Asia heard the word of the Lord.' (Acts 19:10). The letter to the Ephesians, written perhaps some six to eight years later (59-61 A.D.) would have been to all those in the region who responded to the Word of God, a group which extended beyond the bounds of the city of Ephesus.

Luke tells us that Paul's ministry was associated with extraordinary miracles, perhaps a step above the usual apostolic expectation (2 Cor. 12:12). It may have been the particular adherence of some to the cult of the day which necessitated greater displays of divine power. Certainly it seems possible that some professed faith before being confronted with the real power of the gospel: following the experience of the seven sons of Sceva, who sought to invoke the name of Jesus in an attempt to exorcise, many of those who believed 'now came and openly confessed their evil deeds' (Acts 19:18). Presumably prior to this incident they had 'believed' without experiencing the power of the gospel or the need to repent.

As Paul prepared to leave Ephesus, Luke provides us with an account of the city-wide riot instigated by Demetrius the silversmith. He had become aware that the gospel was taking root and that Paul had 'led astray large numbers of people here in Ephesus and practically the whole province of Asia.' (Acts 19:26). The uproar which followed was marked by great confusion (some people did not even know why they were there; Acts 19:32) and perhaps just as much anti-Jewish as anti-Christian sentiment (as was seen by their response to Alexander the Jew). The fact that the officials protected Paul and the city clerk brought peace to the situation suggests that Luke's purpose in recounting this incident was clearly apologetic or political. He wanted to show that Rome had no case against Christianity in particular or Paul in general.'[3]

What is clear from the book of Acts is that by the time Paul left, everyone in Ephesus and the wider province of Asia had heard the gospel and many people, both Jews and Greeks, had believed. Churches had been planted and leaders had been appointed, so much so that when we next hear about Paul and the church in Ephesus, it is in the context of his exhortation to the Ephesian elders.

About a year has passed since Paul left Ephesus and now he arrives down the coast at Miletus, from where he summons the Ephesian elders. Acts 20:25-35 is the only speech in Acts directly to a Christian audience and overwhelmingly it concerns the health of the church in the region. The leaders must watch themselves and the flock of which the Holy Spirit has made them overseers. Negatively, they must be on their guard from false teachers who will emerge even from their own number. Positively, they must hold on to God and the Word of his grace, which can build them up and give them an inheritance among those who are sanctified (Acts 20:30-32).

After Paul's departure the church in Ephesus has a mixed history. He later encourages Timothy to stay in Ephesus in order that he may 'command certain men not

3   J.R.W.Stott, *The Bible Speaks Today, Acts* (Nottingham, UK: IVP, 1990) p. 311.

to teach false doctrines any longer' (1 Tim. 1:3), concerned as he is that people may know how to conduct themselves in God's household, the pillar and foundation of the truth (1 Tim. 3:15). It must have been extremely painful for Paul to see what happened to this fledgling church. As he writes his second letter to Timothy, revealing something more of the challenge for all churches in the last days, he reminds us that 'everyone in the Province of Asia has deserted me ... at my first defence no-one came to my support' (2 Tim. 1:15; 4:16).

Clearly the warnings of Acts 20 were needed and to a certain extent they were heeded. By the time we get to the book of Revelation the words of the risen Lord Jesus to the church in Ephesus suggest that the church is doctrinally pure and discerning; but now their problem had changed. They had lost their first love, they had failed to do the things they did at first; their evangelistic heart had gone cold.

As we survey the New Testament to see what happened to the church in Ephesus and in the province of Asia it makes for sobering reading. The gospel went out, faithfully proclaimed through patient daily ministry, so that all in the province of Asia heard the Word of the Lord. Jews and Gentiles became Christians; pastor-teachers were appointed and charged to keep teaching and keep watch. Their tears of friendship and concern for Paul gave no indication that things would ever change, except that is, for Paul's solemn warning ... 'even from your own number men will arise and distort the truth in order to draw away disciples after them' (Acts 20:30). Later, Timothy had to be left in the region to command such teachers to keep quiet. The church prevailed but lost her first love; and today the church in Ephesus is no more.

Paul's letter picks up all these concerns – the gospel, the need for teaching, the interaction of Christians with one another and the church with the world – and he reminds us of the spiritual warfare in which we are involved, not only as people become part of the church, but as we seek to remain as the church. We have much to learn.

Recipients of the letter

In the light of Paul's experience in Asia Minor, his letter to the Ephesians may well have been designed to be circulated around the churches in Western Asia Minor, centred around the busy city of Ephesus with its population of 250,000. Paul clearly knew at least some of those to whom he was writing (1:16 and 6:19-20) whilst at the same time, he may well have written it with others in mind (see 3:2; 4:21), desiring all Christians to understand the significance of what it meant to be part of God's new community.

The far-reaching implications and universal importance of understanding this truth make it difficult to suggest a particular 'occasion' which generated the letter. Inevitably many suggestions have been made, but perhaps in God's goodness the lack of an obvious setting enables the church of every generation to identify and benefit from these timeless truths. The only 'controversy' or difficulty we discover is the relationship between Jew and Gentile before coming to Christ, and the relationship of the church with the world after people have come to Christ. Such concerns need not be generated by particular historical situations but remain battles and challenges for all God's people, even if the nature of the barriers and difficulties may have changed with time.

The message of Ephesians

We must always hesitate to use a single verse to sum up a letter when the author chose to use many more words to convey his message. When we consider that the letter would probably have been read at one sitting to a gathered congregation (of all ages), it seems rather presumptuous to assume we can encapsulate the entire message in one sentence.

At the same time it is quite possible to trace themes in this letter, all of which ultimately relate to who we are in Christ. It is in him that we have every spiritual blessing; in him we have been chosen and raised – and through him we have been made into that one new entity, the church. Here we find ourselves getting to the heart of the letter, for the church of which Christians are now a part, that strange collection of professing believers who gather together, is a visual aid, a picture of what God has done in the 'heavenly realms.'

We are told in the first chapter that God has revealed his purposes for history, 'And he made known to us the mystery of his will according to his good pleasure, which he purposed in Christ, to be put into effect when the times will have reached their fulfilment – to bring all things in heaven and on earth together under one head, even Christ' (Eph. 1:9-10).

The end point of history is a church, a group of redeemed people from every nation, tribe, language and tongue, who have been reconciled to God and to one another in Christ, singing his praises for all eternity in a new heaven and new earth. Ephesians teaches us that in some senses this future reality is seen now in the church. Those who have responded to Christ have already been spiritually raised with him to the heavenly realms. There he has authority over all things. He is 'far above all rule and authority, power and dominion and every title that can be given, not only in the present age but in the one to come.' (1:21); and there we have every spiritual blessing.

It is that new identity which radically affects how we live in the 'earthly realm.' Those who were alienated, which in the context of this letter is the Jew and the Gentile, have been reconciled. A new community has been formed with new values and new relationships, so all-encompassing that the rulers and authorities in the heavenly realms look at the church, this new community, and see the manifold wisdom of God in operation (3:10). Here is something new, something profoundly powerful, affecting our relationship with fellow believers, our relationship with the world and our domestic relationships (between husbands and wives, children and parents, slaves and masters).

The church, therefore, in all its wonder, is the present expression of eternity, a demonstration of where history is heading. She has been described as 'God's pilot scheme for the reconciled universe of the future.'[4] But as such, the church is under attack. If it is by our love one for another that the world might see we are disciples of Jesus (John 13:34, 35); if the church thereby becomes the most powerful apologetic for the gospel, then it will be the church which finds herself under attack. No wonder it is so difficult to 'be church.' Our battle to be what we are in Christ is not against flesh and blood, but against the rulers, against the authorities, against the powers of this dark world and against the spiritual forces of evil in the heavenly realms. Satan does not want

---

4   F.F. Bruce, *The Epistle to the Ephesians* (London, UK: Pickering and Inglis, 1961), quoted in O'Brien, *Ephesians*, p. 63.

the church either to be formed (by gospel proclamation) or to live as it should (in gospel ethics). And he does not want the church to live as the church (what we might call 'Gospel living'). And so we need the armour of God, the armour he gives to his Messiah in battle; the armour of Christ. As we put on his armour, as we understand who we are in Christ, so the battle can be won. For Christ has been exalted far above all rule and authority, power and dominion. It is in him that the battle to be the church is won. No wonder Paul is so keen to make it clear that we have every spiritual blessing in Christ and that we have been raised with him. We can be the church and we understand the significance of our identity being in him.

And so Ephesians does have a single theme, from which many implications flow; a theme of what it means to be the church, in Christ, reconciled and raised with him; and what that new community, created in the heavenly realms, should look like in the earthly realm. 'A proper understanding of God's intention in Christ has to do with each of these two spheres and what is represented by them, as well as the bond between the two.'[5]

It is wonderfully heartening to know that the churches of which we are a part and within which we minister are not the irrelevant rumps that society would have us believe, but a profound picture of where history is heading and a living apologetic for the gospel. When we unlock Ephesians we set the church on fire.

The principalities and powers

In the light of what we read in the book of Acts, and with the powerful imagery of the warfare in which we are engaged in Ephesians 6:10-20, it is legitimate to ask whether Paul had

5   O'Brien, *Ephesians*, p. 60.

his experiences of the Artemis cult in Ephesus in mind as he wrote about the principalities and powers which fight against the church of Jesus Christ. It is certainly the case, as F.F. Bruce points out, that 'Paul's healing the sick and demon possessed in the name of Jesus provoked opposition and competition from those whose empowerment came from a widely different source. Ephesus was renowned as a centre of the magical arts.'[6] Homer is known to have called Artemis 'mistress of wild beasts,' which perhaps explains Paul's comments in 1 Corinthians 15:32, 'If I fought wild beasts in Ephesus for merely human reasons, what have I gained?' But equally, it is strange how little Paul refers to principalities and powers in this way in his subsequent writing.

The nature of opposition in Ephesus clearly came initially because people were coming to Christ. As those who were previously under the authority of Satan (as in Eph. 2:1-3) become Christians, a cosmic and spiritual event was taking place, as indeed happens whenever people become Christians. The book of Revelation reminds us that the beast 'was given power to make war against the saints and to conquer them, and he was given authority over every tribe, people, language and nation. All inhabitants of the earth will worship the beast – all those whose names have not been written in the book of life' (Rev. 13:7-8). Despite a different background and occasion for writing, this is still written for the church in Ephesus; whose responsibility it is to be witnesses in the world. As the gospel is proclaimed to the world under Satan's authority, so those from every nation, tribe, people and language (7:9) will respond. The

---

6   F.F. Bruce, *The Book of Acts* (GrandRapids, USA: Eerdmans, 1988) p. 410.

enemy is conquered by the proclamation of the gospel (12:11).

In Ephesians the church clearly has that same responsibility as it engages in a fallen world; and to that extent the powers which are confronted by the gospel are those at the command of Satan – powers which can only be overcome by being in Christ. It is also true, as in Revelation, that what threatens the church is the attack of Satan – but what Paul focuses on in order to correct that is not the power of the Artemis cult (a particular manifestation of Satan's warfare), but rather the power of the gospel and the Word to bring about true growth in the church. His warnings to the Ephesians elders do not relate to Artemis and to the spiritual power associated with the cult, but rather to false teaching – which is clearly far more likely to do real damage to the church. His instruction to Timothy is to silence false teachers and to instruct the church so that she can be the church. Likewise, within the letter to the Ephesians Chapter 4 plays a key role in explaining how the Word equips Christians to serve so that, as they serve, the church grows to unity and maturity.

Despite the Demetrius-inspired civil revolt, there is no indication in Acts that the church suffered very much from it. The senior civil leaders not only appear to have supported Paul but also to have silenced the rioters. The church was growing beforehand and, as far as we know, it was growing afterwards. There is no report by the elders at Miletus that the Artemis cult was an on-going problem. Paul's real concern was the danger from within the church rather than from without.

As we study the letter it is evident that Satan is the one from whose authority the gospel rescues people. It is also clear that he seeks to attack that which God has made by the gospel; and whilst this is seen in Ephesus through what happened in connection with the Artemis cult, we would not want to view the whole letter through that particular lens and assume that whenever Paul mentions spiritual powers they relate to a pagan experience which will not touch most of us in the twenty-first century.

Authorship

Questions about authorship should not dominate our thinking as much as they dominate the introduction of many commentaries, but we cannot overlook the question if only because many who seek to teach and preach the letter may have already had the question raised through other studies.

Clearly at the outset of the letter the author identifies himself as the apostle Paul (1:1;3:1). He has personal knowledge of the Ephesians and addresses his ministry and this letter to their situation (1:15-16; 3:1; 4:1; 6:19-20). We would therefore need to have reasonable and considerable evidence to align ourselves with the doubters (who first emerged at the end of the eighteenth and beginning of the nineteenth century). Their arguments were based around the apparently impersonal nature of the letter, which lacks the personal farewell of many other letters, the presence of some unique words in the text, an emphasis on the exaltation of Christ (the so-called 'Cosmic' theology of the letter), the emphasis on the church and the evident similarities with Colossians.

All these objections to Pauline authenticity need not unsettle us. The letter may have been designed to have been circulated around believers in South West Asia (the words 'in Ephesus' in 1:1 are absent from some of the best manuscripts), thereby reducing the need for personal comment; the pool of words used is thought by many to be too insufficient to reject authorship; the theological emphasis, both in its cosmic dimensions and in explanation of the church, is entirely fitting to the issues addressed; and the similarity or dependence on Colossians would be understandable if the heart of the gospel message, as it relates to those 'in Christ', is being proclaimed. There is much theology in common with Paul's other letters, but as with all his correspondence, the purpose or shape and content of each letter is controlled by the issues addressed. Real theology does not occur in a vacuum; it seeks to grow real people in Christian maturity and godliness.

2

IDEAS FOR PREACHING OR TEACHING A SERIES ON EPHESIANS

Different churches will organise preaching rotas in different ways. Where possible, I think it is helpful for the same person to preach through the whole letter. Alternatively, it can be very helpful to have a preaching group where the letter is studied together in order to understand what it means. There is likely to be less confusion if everyone who preaches understands the message.

Too many preachers approach a passage without reference to the rest of the letter. At best this reduces preaching to a series of doctrinal statements which, although possibly true and valid, do not get to the heart of what Paul intended. At worst, such sermons can be erroneous. It is helpful to remember that chapters and verses were added later, that NIV subtitles (which are not always helpful) were added later still and that Bibles with notes do not provide short-cuts to understanding. Sadly many people, keen to learn, refer to the study notes at the bottom of the page rather than the text. This can make it hard for preachers and small group leaders to faithfully expound and apply the text.

When Ephesians was first written it was presumably delivered in its entirety and was not broken up into small sections and studied over several weeks. It was also written for, and probably read to, the whole church (including parents and children, slaves and masters), all of whom would have seen how it was applied to them. To that end, it may be advisable to have an introductory sermon which enables people to see the whole before it is broken into parts. This can be particularly helpful when church members miss a Sunday or so, which seems to happen increasingly.

Preparation

All of us are tempted to head for the commentaries before doing the work on the text ourselves. When Ephesians was first written there were no commentaries and the people for whom the letter was written did not need them. Some of our reliance on commentaries is in fact a symptom of laziness on our part. We think we can short-cut the time required to understand the words of the Bible. But we cannot. We need to work very hard at the text, reading and re-reading it until we are as clear as we can be. When we are confused or uncertain, it can be helpful to read a commentary or two in order that we might better understand the text.

For any preacher the first stage is to read the whole letter several times and to pray for understanding and for those to whom we will speak. The primary prayer is not 'what do these people need to hear?' but rather 'what does this text say?' God knows what people need to hear, which is why he has given us the Bible. People will all be at different stages in their understanding and will have different levels of clarity and confusion in their thinking, which is where sensitivity to what people need to hear is required, but God has given us the letter in its entirety for his church. Our job is to set it forth plainly.

When I prepare, after reading the letter thoroughly I write out the passage to be preached, word for word, usually typed with spaces between each verse. Then, keeping the Bible open I try to see how the part fits with the whole, allowing the structure of the passage to determine the structure of the sermon.

From this, the points which need to be taught should emerge naturally, although we will have a choice as to how we present them: as a summary of the point or as a headline for the point. I find points which ask questions less helpful and points which contain that which people want to remember more helpful. But this is a personal choice and depends on the level of familiarity with the congregation as well as the style of the preacher. The Bible says very little about preaching style even though it is very clear about preaching content.

Having worked out the main body of the sermon and the preaching points I then write the conclusion before finally thinking about the introduction. At first I do try not to think about the congregation to whom I will be preaching, but of the congregation who first heard the letter. As I understand what it meant for them, I shall better understand what it means for us. The congregations to which we preach are the secondary hearers of the letter. If we fail to understand what the primary hearers understood we will be in danger of misunderstanding or misrepresenting the text; we will also be in danger of only saying what itching ears want to hear.

It may be helpful to supply notes with headings so that people can follow the sermon. At times it can also be of great help to run a preaching series in parallel with a Home Group series, but the leaders will still need to be very clear and well taught. Running a home group can be more perilous than preaching because those within the group are able to speak; and those who are most powerful in sharing their thoughts are not always those who are most clear in their thinking.

Dividing the text

There is great danger and great temptation for those of us who preach and teach the Bible to approach the text as if the section from which we are preaching was written in isolation from the rest of the letter. Chapter and verse divisions can be very helpful but they can also be potentially dangerous. Ephesians was not written to be broken down into a series of sermons or studies and the danger of doing so is that we fail to see how the letter itself shapes the parts into which we have chosen to divide it. We struggle for applications without always remembering that the letter has already been applied. Those who first heard it would not have gone home wondering how it applied to them. Having heard it they would have understood and, God willing, acted upon what they heard.

It means that we must always view the part in the light of the whole, remembering that any division we make is, in some senses, a false division, constructed through history or via Bible translation committees. Such structuring is inevitable if we are to digest the material, but we must never forget that whilst a particular jigsaw piece of the letter may teach us much, it is designed as part of a picture which we, the preachers, must see in its fullness if we are to make sense of the part.

To that end, it would be helpful at this point to put this book down and read Ephesians, preferably out loud, thinking all the time of how it would have been heard had we been there in first century Ephesus. How would it have changed us had we been a Jew or a Gentile, a husband, a wife, a child, a slave or a master? Only when we begin to put ourselves in the shoes of those who first heard this letter will we begin to make sense of it and to see the picture in its fullness. And only then will we be ready to examine each piece of the puzzle.

Ideas for preaching or teaching a series on Ephesians

The length of a series will depend again on the nature of the church and what people are used to. On two occasions I have attempted to cover all of Ephesians in two sessions, both at conferences, which is almost impossible, but can serve to give a feel for the letter and draw out some ways it challenges us. I have also preached it at church weekends away in four or five sessions and at an overseas conference for preachers in ten sessions. In our local church we covered the letter in eight sermons.

The shorter series listed below focus on key parts of the letter, giving an overview, but also miss substantial sections, which the preacher may wish to make references to in the sermons.

Four sermons

1	1:3-14
2	2:1-22
3	4:1-6:9
4	6:10-20

Five sermons

1	1:3-14
2	2:1-22
3	4:1-17
4	4:25-6:9
5	6:10-20

Six sermons

1	1:1-14
2	1:15-23
3	2:1-22
4	3:1-21
5	4:1-6:9
6	6:10-20

There are positives and negatives in taking the so-called ethical section of 4:1-6:9 in one block. Positively, it is easier to see how this fits in with the teaching of Ephesians. Negatively, some of the detail will inevitably be lost. By spreading the series out over seven or eight weeks the ethical section can be broken down, either as the three units outlined in this book or by focusing more clearly on one or two sections in more depth. It is also possible to fill the 'gaps' with Home Group material and thus cover more of the letter without increasing the length of the series.

A longer series might consist of ten sermons:

Ten sermons

1	1:1-14
2	1:15-23

3	2:1-22
4	3:1-21
5	4:1-24
6	4:25-5:2
7	5:3-21
8	5:22-33
9	6:1-9
10	6:10-20

For the purpose of this book, I have used an outline of 15 sermons or studies (combining the first two sermons into one chapter). The epistle is so rich that this seems the most faithful approach to preaching or teaching it.

Sixteen sermons

1	1:1-2	Introduction
2	1:3-14	Every blessing in Christ
3	1:15-23	Making it possible
4	2:1-10	A mammoth task (I)
5	2:11-22	A mammoth task (II)
6	3:1-13	How important is the church?
7	3:14-21	It is possible
8	4:1-16	How to be mature
9	4:17-24	Don't be a sinner. Be a saint
10	4:25-5:2	Relationships in the church: be like God
11	5:3-14	Relationships with the world: be light

Part 2
PREACHING OR TEACHING A SERIES ON EPHESIANS

I

EVERY BLESSING IN CHRIST (1:1-14)

In his commentary on Ephesians, John Stott introduces us to John Mackay, the former president of Princeton Theological Seminary. As a young man his life was turned upside down by reading Paul's letter to the Ephesians, for there he discovered the centrality and magnitude of Christ. 'Jesus Christ became the centre of everything,' he said. 'I had been quickened; I was really alive.'[1] Later, when invited to deliver the Croall Lectures in Edinburgh in 1947, he chose to expound this great letter, referring to it as 'pure music ... what we read here is truth that sings, doctrine set to music.'[2]

Even a cursory reading of the first fourteen verses of the letter will give us some understanding of what Mackay experienced in his own life and later sought to convey in his preaching. These introductory words set the tone for the whole letter. Densely packed with Christian doctrine, they are wide in their portrayal of salvation history and almost

1   J.R.W. Stott, *The Bible Speaks Today: Ephesians* (Nottingham, UK: IVP, 1979) p. 15.
2   Stott, *Ephesians*, p. 16.

poetic in their presentation. They take us on a tour of God's purposes in Christ, from before the foundation of the world to his future inheritance in the new heaven and the new earth. We would do well to pause in prayer and reflection, humbly digesting these great truths before we take up the surgeon's knife in preparation for our preaching. These are words which must first and foremost glorify God.

Preliminary observations

After his initial introduction, Paul breaks into a wonderful hymn of praise running as one long continual sentence of 202 words from verses 3-14. Many commentators have sought to impose a structure on it, but helpfully for us no general consensus has been reached. We have the text as it is and we must make sense of it as it stands.

Certain features can be seen to shape this eulogy:

+ The focus is clearly the praise of God for his blessings. Verses 3-14 begin with praise: *Praise be to God* and end with praise *to the praise of his glory*. Within these bookends of praise we see the nature of the work of God from before the foundation of the world to our future inheritance in glory. God's purposes, past, present and future, are set out for us.

+ The spheres in which we experience and enjoy God's blessings are 'in Christ' and 'in the heavenly realms'. All the gifts between verses 3-14 are part of this package of blessing and are therefore grounds for giving praise to God.

+ The way in which the blessings are experienced is through the agency of the Holy Spirit: the blessings are from God, in Christ, mediated by the Spirit.

In these verses we have the plan and purposes of God unfolded for us. What was hidden has now been made known; the purposes of God in history are no longer a secret. God's purposes in Christ are 'to be put into effect when the times have reached their fulfilment – to bring all things in heaven and on earth together under one head, even Christ' (1:9-10).

There is also a hint in these verses of what is yet to come in the rest of the letter. As the nature and sphere of God's blessings are explained and his purposes for history are revealed, so also the present outworking of that is now being seen in the church. The end of the eulogy praises God for the emergence of a new community, made up of Jew and Gentile who together share the promise of the future and who will display a picture of that future in their lives together.

Listening to the text

(1) Paul, an apostle of Christ Jesus by the will of God, to the saints in Ephesus, the faithful in Christ Jesus: (2) Grace and peace to you from God our Father and the Lord Jesus Christ. (3) Praise be to the God and Father of our Lord Jesus Christ, who has blessed us in the heavenly realms with every spiritual blessing in Christ. (4) For he chose us in him before the creation of the world to be holy and blameless in his sight. In love (5) he predestined us to be adopted as his sons through Jesus Christ – (6) to the praise of his glorious grace, which he has freely given us in the one he loves. (7) In him we have redemption through his blood, the forgiveness of sins, in accordance with the riches of God's grace, (8) that he lavished on us with all wisdom and understanding. (9) And he made known to us the mystery of his will according to his good pleasure,

which he purposed in Christ, (10) to be put into effect when the times will have reached their fulfilment – to bring all things in heaven and on earth together under one head, even Christ. (11) In him we were chosen, having been predestined according to the plan of him who works out everything in conformity with the purpose of his will, (12) in order that we, who were the first to hope in Christ, might be for the praise of his glory. (13) And you also were included in Christ when you heard the word of truth, the gospel of your salvation. Having believed, you were marked in him with a seal, the promised Holy Spirit, (14) who is a deposit guaranteeing our inheritance until the redemption of those who are God's possession – to the praise of his glory.

Introductions (1:1-2)
Although adopting what was no more than the usual style of greeting for ancient letter writing, Paul begins his letter with powerful hints as to what the rest of the letter might contain. The fact that Paul is an apostle not only reminds us that he has been 'sent', but also that he is uniquely qualified to be the bearer of the gospel of Jesus Christ (2:20; 3:5). He is operating as a servant of King Jesus. It is by the will of God that he proclaims this message.

The recipients of the letter are described as 'saints', those who have been made holy and, indeed, as we read the letter, those who are expected and empowered to live increasingly holy lives. In the mixed pagan culture of Ephesus, it is their faith, given by God, which enables them to be part of this new community and to live as light in a dark world.

This God-given message which creates the church is mediated by grace and it is by grace that the church which the message produces comes about (1:6,7; 2:5, 7, 8; 3:2, 7, 8;

4:7; 6:24). Likewise the peace which is from 'God our Father and the Lord Jesus Christ' is a peace which is mediated to them in the making of the church and experienced in them as they live as the church (2:14, 15, 17; 4:3; 6:15, 23).

At this stage the full implications of these words have not been spelled out and we would do well in our preaching to think carefully about whether at this stage we would preach these verses. It may be more profitable to refer back to them in later sermons as the implication and weight of each word become apparent. Our work in the study may confirm the importance of them as we see their connection with what follows, but if the sermon is to live and be more than an academic exercise, we may be wise to hold our fire.

Every spiritual blessing in Christ (1:3)

Here, in this wonderful expression of praise, we are introduced to a term which is both unique to Ephesians and fundamental to it. The 'heavenly realms', or 'heavenlies', appears a number of times (1:3, 20; 2:6; 3:10; 6:12). A cursory reading of the way in which the term is used might initially confuse us. It is the sphere of our blessing (1:3), the place to which Christ has been raised (1:20), the place to which the believer has also been raised spiritually (2:6); the view-point from which the rulers and authorities look at the church (3:10) and the place of spiritual warfare and conquest (6:12).

When we put these verses together we can see that the heavenly realms are where the principalities and powers are located, over which the risen Jesus has higher and total authority not only in the present age but also in the one to come. He has been placed there and given all authority, we are told, for the church (1:20).

We are clearly not yet in the heavenly realms physically. The Ephesians, like us, would have known only too well some of the reality of what life is like in the earthly realms. Indeed, the letter is written so that we might increasingly express here what we have been made there, as we head towards that day when all things in heaven and on earth are brought together under one head, Christ.

When preaching 1:3 we may need to explain a little of what Ephesians says about this realm, even if the full explanation is not given at this stage. Our first section does not give everything we might want to know, and we must therefore be careful not to preach all of Ephesians at the first bite, but it might be helpful for those to whom we are preaching to know that the heavenly realm is the place where Christ now resides, with all authority.

Praise for election and adoption (the past blessings)(1:4-6)
The nature and benefits of these blessings now start to be unfolded (the verse begins with 'even as' or 'for') as we are taken behind the curtain of history. God's purpose in making a people finds its origins not in those who choose to become a part of that people, but in his intentions before the foundation of the world. It is all from him.

His purpose and intention for his people is that we would be holy and blameless and loving (see Rom. 8:29). Without the benefits of sentence breaks it can be difficult to know whether 'in love' of verse 4 should go with the first part of verse 4 (in which case God chose us to be holy, blameless and loving) or the first part of verse 5 (in which case God's motive in choosing us was love). However, on balance it seems more likely that Paul meant to make a statement about the people God was creating. Later he will instruct the church to 'live a life of love' modelled on the

Lord Jesus – that is what God wants from his people. He is making a people who will present eternity to the world (a place where the love of people will be perfected as we bask in the glory of the God who is love).

But this new people will not relate to God out of duty but as his children. We are predestined to be adopted as sons. For the Jew, sonship would have been identified with the privileges of Israel (Exod. 4:22; Isa. 1:2; Hosea 11:1). For the Gentile, the Graeco-Roman practice of adoption might have been in mind. Either way, here was something new. This was written to all the saints, the Christians, together – both Jew and Gentile. Now a new people will relate to him as sons, through Christ, because of God's will and pleasure, and therefore inevitably, to the praise of his glorious grace.

As we come to the end of verse 6 and move to verse 7 we see the purposes of God break into the plane of human history. Once again, all is in Christ (in the one he loves) and thoroughly undeserved (he has freely given it).

It may be worth having in mind the fact that many people hold an incomplete understanding of what God intended to do in his world. Before the fall God planned a people who would be perfected in Christ. Eden, even before the fall, was not God's ultimate intention. He intended a new people perfected in Christ in a new heaven and a new earth. Eden is an essential part of that purpose but not its climax.

Praise for redemption and forgiveness (present blessings)(1:7-8)

As we enter the stage of human history, the tense of the verbs changes. In the past God had chosen us, predestined us and adopted us. Now, because of Christ *we have* redemption and forgiveness. These, along with knowledge of the gospel and the down-payment of the Spirit, are present realities for the Christian; and they have been achieved through the blood of Jesus.

All three terms here – blood, redemption and the forgiveness of sins – are loaded with Old Testament meaning but are not fully explained here. Whilst reference is made to the effect of the cross, the mechanism of atonement is not explained. It must be assumed that a) the Ephesian church had sufficient understanding of what Paul meant by these terms and b) that the cross is essential to form the church (Paul does explain the centrality of the cross in 2:14-16) but it is not the main focus of the letter. It may be reasonable to assume that, like many churches today, it is possible for believers to articulate a theology of the cross clearly without grasping its implication for the way in which we relate to each other as the church.

What is unexpected is the phrase 'with all wisdom and understanding.' We do not naturally think that wisdom and understanding relate to redemption and forgiveness, but without a right understanding of the cross we cannot have wisdom and understanding to live as God's people.

Praise for God's future plan for the world (future blessings) (1:9-10)

In the Bible the word 'mystery' is not used of something which cannot be understood, but rather of something which has not been disclosed. Paul tells us that the mystery, the hidden secret has been made known: God's will, purposed in Christ, seen in fullness at the end of time, is to bring all things in heaven and on earth under one head, who is Christ.

Here we see the two 'realms', which run as strands throughout this letter, being brought together. We have already been introduced to the heavenly realms in verse 3.

Now the earthly realm is introduced, the place in which we now live (see also 1:10; 3:15; 4:9; 6:3). God's purpose in history, that to which all we see and experience is heading, relates to the rule of Christ. The great surprise of this revealed mystery is that God is making a new people, comprised of Jew and Gentile, those who were previously alienated; and that both will share together in the promise of Christ Jesus (3:5-6).

That may not seem much to us, until we realise just how alienated those two groups were. Our studies in chapter 2 will shed more light on the gulf between the two groups and the wonderful grace of God in bringing them together. For now we need to note that the focal point of history is Jesus Christ and a people gathered round him. He is not simply the means of becoming part of this new people; he is our head and our focus.

What should surprise us as we read on is that God has begun this process already, in the earthly realm, as he has brought Jew and Gentile together through the gospel. The Gospel brings the future into the present.

Praise for a new people and shared inheritance (1:11-14)

As we read these verses, which are still part of our long, original sentence, we notice that there is a distinction between the 'we' of verses 11 and 12 and the 'you' of verse 13. By the time we come to the end of the section, in verse 14, we discover that the inheritance is 'ours.'

The Jews were always regarded as God's people. The gospel was promised to them, having been announced in advance to Abraham (Gal. 3:8); it was first for them and then for the Gentiles (Rom. 1:16). In the Song of Moses (Deut. 32:8-9), God's people are referred to as his 'portion' or inheritance. (Hence ESV 1:11 'In him we have obtained an inheritance'.) Those Jews who were the first to hope in Christ were the faithful remnant who believed his promises. They were his inheritance; their salvation was to the praise of his glory.

But what is wonderful, and extraordinary, is that through the gospel (the revealed mystery of God), the Gentiles can also be included in this new people as they hear the Word of truth and believe (v. 13). And so the glory which goes to God in praise as the Jews become believers in the Lord Jesus (v. 12) is mirrored as the Gentiles are included (v. 14).

There is now a new people with a new inheritance, hinted at in verses 9-10 and seen worked out in the present reality of the church. The guarantor of that inheritance is the Spirit, given as a deposit of what is yet to come. It is as we are filled with him (the Spirit) that we can live now as new people (see notes on 5:18f), displaying to the principalities the wisdom of God, and to the world the power of the gospel. As we shall discover throughout Ephesians, Gospel power is seen in the formation of the church and in the living of the church. Neither would be possible without the initiative of God, mediated by Christ and experienced through the transforming work of the Spirit.

From text to teaching

So far, the text has not asked anything of its hearers. There is no command or point of action. However, this passage is overflowing with praise which comes from a right understanding of what God has done for us in Christ. As we preach it, that must be the response we desire from those who listen. We long for the response of praise to God for his overwhelming goodness to us in Christ Jesus.

We have noted that the tightly packed, single-sentence nature of this passage (vv. 3-14) has made consensus as to the structure of the passage difficult. When we cannot detect an obvious structure to a passage it may mean that the text can be legitimately preached in a number of ways. Much of what we read in this eulogy is explained and amplified throughout the letter and there will be time in a series to come back to the truths we discover. It is like an overture to the letter, and we will hear the tune again; and as we listen more it will become easier to understand and so we do not need to include all that we have discovered in the study.

It would be wise to start with 1:3 which tells us the direction of our praise and the reason for our praise. Thereafter we can explain what God has done in Christ.

Introduction

Sermon introductions should always be written last, after we have prepared the rest of the sermon. Without knowing where we are going we cannot start our journey. Introductions may arrest or challenge; they may open the hearer to questions which hitherto had not been entertained. They should touch the real experience of those who hear so that there is a drive and impetus to change thinking, to be rebuked, corrected, challenged or encouraged.

In this passage, the dominant feature of praise is focused ultimately on the formation of a new people, the church. As most of us have very mixed experiences of church and tend to be over-individualistic in our view of salvation, the shock factor of verses 3-14 is that praise is directed towards God for what he has done in Christ in making the church. That surprise can provide a helpful way in to the sermon.

Preaching outline – an example

If we are to keep the focus on praise then it is important that we understand the realities that drive that praise. To that end, the following headings might serve to direct our hearers into the mind of Paul and the heart of God:

1. Praise God - You lack nothing (1:3)

2. Chosen to be a perfect people (1:4-6)

3. Chosen through the cross (1:7-8)

4. Praise God – You are a picture of the future (1:9-14)

This structure aims to 'wrap' the sermon in praise, following the bookends of praise in verse 3 and verse 14. The titles make sense only in the light of an introduction about the church. I have worded the first title 'you lack nothing' because the drive of the whole letter is that we can be the people we are made to be. Whilst this is not explained fully in 1:1-14, our hearers need to know that we have everything we need to be the church because we have been given every spiritual blessing in Christ, in the heavenly realms.

God has chosen us in Christ to be a perfect people. Again, because the letter takes us to the outworking of this, we need to keep an 'Ephesian feel' to each sermon. As this is all from God, this is possible.

The means by which we have been chosen and made this people is through the blood of Christ. Only in him do we have redemption, forgiveness, and only through his death are we able to have the wisdom and understanding to be the church (as is made clear in chapter 2).

When we have been made the church (here the Jew/Gentile issue can be introduced) we become a picture of what God is doing in eternity. Verses 9-10 are therefore linked to 1:11-14 and presented as that which is then unpacked throughout the letter.

An alternative approach would be to focus on the nature of the blessings lavished upon us in Christ and how they are related to our past, present and future (as suggested by the sub-divisions within this chapter). A sermon structured in this way might then be presented as follows:

- Praise God for the past blessings of election (1:4-6)

- Praise God for the present blessings of redemption (1:7-8)

- Praise God for the future blessings of completion (1:9-10)

- You are part of a glorious inheritance (1:11-14)

It must be remembered that the focus in the letter is very much on God and on what he has done in Christ to make the church. It is a message which is not always easy to hear within our individualistic Western culture and we would be wise to do what we can to maintain that 'feel' as we plan our sermons. That said, there might be a place for taking the four titles used above and using them more directly. We might, for example, simply title the whole sermon 'four reasons to praise God.' Whatever we do, we need both to handle the text carefully and also to be aware of the confusion and concern which might arise in connection with the doctrines of election, predestination and the nature of the church. Some of these may need to be unpacked as we go; others will be better dealt with by letting the text of the letter speak in subsequent sermons.

Application

I find it helpful to make a distinction between application and implication. The Bible is already applied; the application of this passage is given later in the letter. However, there are implications for this applied truth. These will vary from congregation to congregation and can only be worked out when we have understood the application to the congregation to whom the letter was first addressed.

In this first section, we find ourselves focusing on praise, which comes as we understand what God has done for us in Christ, not only individually (which is not the focus of Ephesians) but corporately. God's purpose in Christ is that he is making a new people.

There are, however, clear challenges in this first part of the letter:

+ The church comes about by God's initiative

+ We can only understand who we are and be who we are by means of the cross.

+ The church is a picture of the future, which we can experience now, in part, by the Spirit.

Questions for home groups/study groups

Introductory Questions

1. What confidence and expectation do we have as we read the opening verses of Ephesians (1:1-2)? (See 3:4-6)

2. Describe Jesus according to 1:19-22.

3. How does this relate to the believer? (See 2:6)

4. In the light of this, what does it mean to say that the believer 'has been blessed in the heavenly realms with every spiritual blessing in Christ'? (1:3)

5. How might this affect our thinking and behaviour? (It is helpful to think about how these truths were expected to affect the Ephesians e.g. 4:1, 17, 25-32.)

Studying the passage

1. What has God done for the believer?

2. By what means has he done it?

3. Given what we know about humanity from Ephesians (2:1-3), why is it so important to know that God has chosen us?

4. From our perspective, how do we become a part of what God is doing?

5. From these verses, what does the Christian have in the present?

6. How does this affect our future?

7. How would you explain the difference between what the Christian already has and what is yet to come?

8. Explain why Paul uses 'we', 'you' and 'our' in verses 11-13.

9. In what way have these verses changed your thinking? (About God, Jesus, the Holy Spirit, yourself, the church?)

10. How might this passage change the way you behave this week?

2

MAKING IT POSSIBLE (1:15-23)

It was J.C. Ryle, the first Bishop of Liverpool, who is reported to have said, 'In his Word God reveals his will, and by prayer we ask him to do it.' In the first fourteen verses Paul has reminded us that God has revealed his will; indeed more than that, he has revealed his whole plan for the history of the world, seen now in the extraordinary and wonderful formation of a new people, the church.

Having presented this glorious eulogy, Paul then moves to prayer, with the hope and expectation that what is true of us may be seen in us, by the power and grace of God.

Preliminary observations

Ephesians contains two main sections of prayer (1:15-23 and 3:14-21), both of which begin with the phrase 'for this reason.' Although the wording is slightly different in the original Greek, it is clear that Paul is driven to pray as a result of the doctrine he has just explained. Prayer serves to bring the truth of God into the hearts, lives and experience of God's people.

If we assume that the eulogy is in some ways an introduction, or overture, to the letter, then we will see that the two prayers are also strategically placed before the two great teaching sections of the letter. The first relates to Paul's explanation of how the church (the 'new man') came into being, and the second relates to how we now live as the church. Prayer is therefore an essential ingredient in making these truths a reality. God has revealed his will – and by prayer Paul asks him to do it.

That must inform our preaching and our praying. As we prepare, we must pray that the truths which are proclaimed do not remain as lifeless doctrine. Knowledge that does not result in changed living leads only to pride and religious arrogance. Truth which is rightly taught and rightly heard leads to godliness. And so for ourselves and for those to whom we minister, prayer must be at the heart of all we do and preach.

But we must also take note of the fact that these sections on prayer are to be preached. When we encourage others by saying that we will pray for them, we very rarely tell them *what* we will pray for them (perhaps because we are not completely sure ourselves). Here Paul not only tells them he is praying; he also explains the content of his prayer.

We dare not do less. Many people are greatly confused about prayer and wonder why God does not seem to answer their prayers. The truth is that God has only promised to do what he has set out in His Word. Anything else he might graciously choose to do is a bonus or blessing. We would find far fewer disappointed Christians if we taught what the Bible teaches about prayer. God has been very kind in giving us these words, for as we read them we begin to realise what God wants us to pray for his people in order that they would grow and that he would be glorified.

Listening to the text

(15) For this reason, ever since I heard about your faith in the Lord Jesus and your love for all the saints, (16) I have not stopped giving thanks for you, remembering you in my prayers. (17) I keep asking that the God of our Lord Jesus Christ, the glorious Father, may give you the Spirit of wisdom and revelation, so that you may know him better. (18) I pray also that the eyes of your heart may be enlightened in order that you may know the hope to which he has called you, the riches of his glorious inheritance in the saints, (19) and his incomparably great power for us who believe. That power is like the working of his mighty strength, (20) which he exerted in Christ when he raised him from the dead and seated him at his right hand in the heavenly realms, (21) far above all rule and authority, power and dominion, and every title that can be given, not only in the present age but also in the one to come. (22) And God placed all things under his feet and appointed him to be head over everything for the church, (23) which is his body, the fullness of him who fills everything in every way.

Introduction (1:15-16)

Paul's reason for praying relates to all he has explained in his wonderful and richly packed eulogy, but perhaps his prayer is particularly focused on the last two verses of the previous section (vv. 13-14) where he has reminded his readers of the joint inheritance that is theirs (both Jew and Gentile) through the gospel purposes of God. These life-changing truths of the gospel are perhaps already being seen in the Ephesian church. They have faith (something which will be explained more fully in the following section) and 'love towards all the saints.'

The word 'saints' is commonly used to describe Christians, all those who have been and are being sanctified. (1:1; 3:18; 6:18), but it is also sometimes used to describe Jewish believers. In other words, it could be that Paul is thanking God because he has heard that the Gentiles' faith and love ('your' rather than 'our') is towards all the saints (i.e. the Jewish Christians). Even if we feel that is going too far, it is clear that there is already a 'togetherness' among a people who, by all social conventions of the day, should be separate.

Prayer for growth (1:16-19)

Paul is constant in his praying. His knowledge of the sovereignty of God in election and in the guarantee of a future hope for his people does not diminish his burden for prayer. On the contrary, because God has promised it, he is more inclined to pray. His great desire in prayer is for the Ephesians to have a greater grasp of what is already theirs in Christ; and as they know it, to live in the light of it. And so he prays that the God of our Lord Jesus Christ, the glorious Father, might give them the Spirit of wisdom and revelation so that they will know him better.

It is important to realise that God has already revealed his will. The mystery, which was hidden, has now been revealed. God is making a new people in Christ; and in Christ we have every spiritual blessing. There is no more we can have of all that is in Christ, even though we will only experience a part of that fullness while here on earth. Likewise, in Christ, we have all wisdom and understanding (1:8). So Paul is not praying for something new. Rather, he is praying that those who are in Christ might come into a greater understanding of what is already theirs. In particular, there are three areas of 'knowledge' he longs for them to have:

He wants them to know the hope to which God has called them.
Biblical hope is always future certainty rather than wishful
thinking. Paul has already told them that God is in the
business of nudging history on, day by day, to that time when
all things in heaven and on earth will be brought 'together
under one head, even Christ' (1:9, 10). That inheritance
and the fullness of redemption are guaranteed by the Spirit
and will one day be experienced in fullness. Paul longs for
the Ephesian Christians to know what God has promised
and how the church now relates to that promise.

He wants them to know the riches of his glorious inheritance.
At first sight this might seem to be no more than an
alternative way of explaining the future. But whereas in
1:14 Paul wrote of 'our inheritance' (i.e. that which will one
day be ours in the new heaven and the new earth in Christ),
here Paul writes of God's inheritance. Just as his Old
Testament people were his portion or possession (1:14),
so his New Testament people are now his inheritance. It
seems likely then, that Paul is praying for the Ephesians to
understand the significance of what it means to be a part of
God's people, his new creation, this wonderful picture of
eternity, the church. Prayer is required for God's people to
understand the wonder and significance of what it means
to be the church – now and as part of that glorious future
hope. Such understanding does not come naturally.

He wants them to know the power of God to be the church.
'Power' is seen at a number of points in the letter. It is
a notable feature of both prayers, and whenever it is used,
it relates to Gospel revelation and Gospel living. Although
Paul does not 'unpack' that meaning here, we have seen that
he prays in order that they might be the church and might

know God better. As we continue our studies, we will see
the significance of that power and how it works more clearly.

Power for growth (1:20-23)

The power that is available for believers to be the church
has been demonstrated in the physical reality of the
resurrection. Jesus has been raised from the dead and seated
with God in the heavenly realms (where we as believers
have our blessings), far above all rule and authority, power
and dominion and every title that can be given, not only in
the present age but also in the one to come.

We might think it rather strange that Paul gives
a lengthy explanation of where Jesus is at this stage, when
explaining the power of the resurrection. He could have
used far fewer words if he was concerned to explain power
alone. It is only as we read on that we realise the magnitude
of his words, for we discover that the believer has been
raised (spiritually) with Christ (2:6); and the battle we face
to be the church, a battle with the rulers and authorities in
the heavenly realms, can only be fought on the basis of who
we are in Christ. When we realise that he has been raised
above all powers in the heavenly realms and that we have
been raised with him we can begin to see the significance
of understanding our identity in him, especially if we are to
live as the church. In him we have every spiritual blessing;
in him (and his armour) it is possible to stand against
everything which might be thrown at us in Satan's attempt
to stop us being the church, because spiritually we are in
a place which is higher than the authority of Satan.

The power that is available for us is none other than
that which can enable us to stand against Satan, as those in
Christ, and to live the Christian life. Becoming what we are
is possible because of what we are in Christ.

We cannot deal with the entire letter through the excitement of this one prayer, but it does explain why Paul includes the words *for the church* at the end of the chapter. God placed Jesus where he is, in order that we could live as he wants us to live, as the church, his body, literally the *fullness of all things with all things filling.*

This is an important prayer for the church in every generation; a prayer that we might know what we are and become what we are, which is only possible because we have every spiritual blessing in Christ in the heavenly realms. The 'location' of Christ and our spiritual identity mean that it is possible to overcome Satan and be the people God has made us to be.

From text to teaching

Introduction
There are many surprises which serve to introduce a sermon on this passage but, as we preach it, we must keep in mind that Paul's concern is that the Ephesians might know God better. His prayer comes after the wonderful eulogy which culminates in the shock that God's eternal purposes are manifest in the church. And it comes before the section which explains what God has done in Christ to make the church. Our introduction must therefore, in some way, focus on the God-given reality that through his power we can become what we are.

Tempting though it might be to use the introduction to talk about how we should pray biblically, I think it is wiser for us to focus on our experience of church and how we can be church, as Paul does. That is where we are, with all our failings, frustrations and shortcomings. The question that will increasingly form in the minds of those who study

Ephesians is 'is it really possible to be this kind of church, the kind of church that God wants?' Both Paul's prayers in this letter give the answer 'yes.'

Before coming to the main content of the sermon it may be worth noting that the Ephesians are already living as God wants to them to live, at least in part. Although the churches of which we are a part are all far from what we would like them to be, thanksgiving for what we are must not be forgotten. God makes us what we are, even though we are a work in progress. We must thank him.

Preaching outline – an example

1. Know the hope to which God has called us (1:17-18a)

2. Know the people which God has made us (1:18b)

3. Know God's power for those who believe (1:20-23)

Although these are worded as exhortations, it must be remembered that for Paul they form the content of his prayer. Throughout our preaching we need to be cautious of using this section to teach doctrinal truths alone. Paul is praying and an answer to his prayer is possible because these truths are real, but that answer will be seen in lives empowered to live as part of God's people, demonstrating a quality of life and love that the world cannot offer.

With this in mind it may be helpful to introduce the sermon by linking the content of our prayers to God's purpose for the church. For Paul his explanation of the prayer serves to instruct the church about what God wants for the church. We would do well to do the same.

Application
The application of this section must relate to our praying and our living. If we are to live as the church, we need to shape

our praying to confirm to Paul's. We also need to remember that as we pray we can become the people God would have us be. Applications need to be made in such a way that we are both motivated to pray and also empowered to live. At the end of the sermon it might be wise to give more time to pray this prayer, perhaps arranging the prayer time within the gathering to be based on this prayer, both in thanksgiving and intercession.

Questions for home groups/study groups

Many study groups or home groups spend some time in prayer at the end of each study. We can, of course, bring all things to the Lord in prayer, but it is notable how rarely individuals keep their Bibles open so that their prayers might be directed by the passage studied. As we learn more about God we must ask that he would write these truths deeply in our hearts and that our lives would change accordingly.

When it comes to the passages which contain examples of prayer, as this one does, we must be even more disciplined and diligent in ensuring that the content of what we pray is shaped by the passage. Practically, it might be helpful to give each member of the group a sheet of paper with the key aspects of this prayer written out, below which they could write the names of those for whom these truths are being prayed. There may also be some general questions which could be re-visited in the following studies. These might include such questions as: 'In what ways have you got to know God better? In what way has your understanding of the hope to which you have been called increased? In what way has your understanding of what it means to be the church developed?'

It might also be worth posing a question about our experience of God's power; a question which should be answered with increasing clarity as the studies continue and one which should, hopefully, correct much of the misunderstanding that circulates in the minds of many. Revisiting these questions will not only serve to reinforce the message of Ephesians but will also strengthen and direct the church's prayer to be more in line with the nature and expectation of prayer in the New Testament.

Suggested Questions

1. Paul thanks God for the love and faith of the Ephesian church. In what ways do we see the gospel realities of verses 3-14 being worked out in our own church?

2. How does the request for the Spirit of wisdom and revelation relate to 1:3, 7-10?

3. Paul wants his readers to know God better. What three realities does he want us to grasp in order for this to happen?

4. What is the hope to which he has called us? How does it relate to 1:9-10 and 1:14?

5. How is the church described in these verses? How does that differ from the understanding you have of what church is all about?

6. What has God done to demonstrate his power?

7. Where is Jesus now? Why is this important for our understanding of Ephesians?

8. What difference could this prayer make to us as the church?

9. How does this compare to the content of your prayers?

10. How might this prayer shape your praying for the church in the future?

3
A MAMMOTH TASK I (2:1-10)

Ephesians 2:1-10 is perhaps one of the most wonderful and shocking passages of scripture ever written. For here we discover the true diagnosis of humanity – and it is far worse than most of us would like to admit. But we also discover the amazing grace and goodness of God – and it is far greater than any of us could possibly imagine. If we fail to grasp the severity of our sin and the reality of our situation outside Christ, we will never grasp the wonder or the power of the gospel.

It is no accident that we find Paul writing these words immediately after his prayer. He wants the Ephesian Christians to know the incomparably great power for those who believe, a power which was demonstrated in the physical reality of the resurrection of Jesus. Now he reminds them that it was that same power which was required to raise them to the sphere in which they now enjoy the blessings of God – the heavenly realms.

Preliminary observations

The choice of words in the NIV ('As for you') might lead
us to think that Paul is branching out on a new topic, but
a better translation is 'and you' (as in the ESV). This links
what Paul is about to write with what he has just taught
in connection with the power of God. This chapter takes
us to the heart of what God had to do to make the church,
in reconciling mankind to himself (2:1-10) and reconciling
Jew to Gentile (2:11-22). There is a sense in which Paul
wants his readers to know and remember (note the use of
the word in 2:11,12) what they were, to understand the
spiritual significance of being made into the 'new man' with
all the associated blessings of 1:3-14.

Ephesians 2:1-10 is a natural section on which to preach.
For although the two parts of the chapter are linked and
must be understood in their entirety if we are to have a fully
Biblical picture of church, there are also natural 'bookends'
which cradle the passage. Paul begins by reminding the
Ephesians of the way in which they used to 'walk' (2:1) and
ends the section by telling them of the ways in which they
are now able to 'walk.' They have moved from the walk of
death to the walk of life simply because of the wonderful
love and grace of God.

In the original Greek there are two sentences, one from 2:1-7
and the second from 2:8-10. The first of these teaches us about
what God has done. He is the main subject and his activity, to
make alive, is the main verb of the section. The second section
explains how his activity affects our daily living.

Listening to the text

(1) As for you, you were dead in your transgressions and
sins, (2) in which you used to live when you followed the

ways of this world and of the ruler of the kingdom of the air, the spirit who is now at work in those who are disobedient. (3) All of us also lived among them at one time, gratifying the cravings of our sinful nature and following its desires and thoughts. Like the rest, we were by nature objects of wrath. (4) But because of his great love for us, God, who is rich in mercy, (5) made us alive in Christ even when we were dead in transgressions – it is by grace you have been saved. (6) And God raised us up with Christ and seated us with him in the heavenly realms in Christ Jesus, (7) in order that in the coming ages he might show the incomparable riches of his grace, expressed to us in Christ Jesus. (8) For it is by grace you have been saved, through faith – and this not from yourselves, it is the gift of God – (9) not by works, so that no-one can boast. (10) For we are God's workmanship, created in Christ Jesus to do good works, which God prepared in advance for us to do.

What we were – The walk of death (2:1-3)

Throughout the first part of Ephesians the Jew/Gentile distinction is very evident. We noted that in the eulogy Paul reminds his readers that 'we [the Jews] were chosen ... and you also were included'. Likewise here in chapter 2 we see the same pattern. In both 'reconciliations', (of mankind to God and Jew to Gentile) we see the same schema employed. So Paul writes 'As for you, you were dead in transgressions and sins in which you used to live when you followed the ways of this world and of the ruler of the kingdom of the air, the spirit who is now at work in those who are disobedient;' but then he goes on to include all others: 'All of us also lived among them at one time, gratifying the cravings of our sinful nature and following its desires and thoughts.' Although Paul may be addressing a predominately Gentile audience, he wants them and us to know that he is providing the diagnosis of all humanity. No-one can escape, no-one is exempt. Whether we claim a fine religious pedigree, or live a life of pagan debauchery, whether we are Jew or Gentile, this is a description of you and me outside Christ.

We were dead in transgressions and sins.
John Stott makes the useful distinction between these two words. Transgression, he says, is the crossing of a boundary or deviation from a path. It equates with sin of commission. That is, we know what to do and consciously chose to do otherwise. Sin, on the other hand, represents our sin of omission. It is the missing of the mark, the falling short of a target. We may want to live in the right way, we may try to do so, but we find we cannot. The standards we set and the standards God sets are too high. Whether or not we can be so prescriptive, there is no doubt that 'these two words seem to have been carefully chosen to give a comprehensive account of human evil.'[1]

This diagnosis of the human condition is uncomfortable for many, especially when we may claim to live life, enjoy life and even make a contribution to the lives of others. But if Paul can widen this diagnosis to all humanity, which includes the religious and morally upright Jew, then we cannot escape. However righteous we may feel (and it is usually self-righteousness), we are spiritually dead. Were that not the case, then the necessity of God's work in Christ would be diminished or, worse still, become redundant. Paul wants his readers to be very clear about their condition before God in order that they might see more clearly his grace, power and love. His purpose in being so explicit is ultimately so that we understand what God has done to make the church. If we, or others, react negatively to this

1   Stott, *Ephesians*, p. 71.

teaching we rob the gospel of its power and the church of its status as God's people.

We were enslaved

The walk of this world, the walk of transgression and sin, may feel like it is driven by individual choice, but Paul is at pains to explain that the Christ-less world is not free. On the contrary, he speaks of three masters who control us before we are rescued in Christ: the world, the devil and the flesh.

The ways of this world is better translated *according to the age of this world*, in other words, in accordance with the old age as opposed to the new age in Christ. If the new age of Christ is characterised by a different walk (2:10; 4:1; 5:2), then the old age, or the ways of this world, is a pattern of living which is different from and in opposition to the ways of God's new people. We express this rebellion in a number of ways, from polite and acceptable apathy, to overt rebellion and lawlessness. The point Paul is making is that without Christ we walk in the ways of the Christless age.

The Devil is referred to here as the *Ruler of the kingdom of the air*. Elsewhere in the New Testament he is the Prince of demons (Matt. 9:34; 12:24; Mark 3:22; Luke 11:15), the Prince of this world (John 12:31; 14:30; 16:11) and the God of this age (2 Cor. 4:4), but it is clear that Paul is speaking about the Devil. He will appear again in 4:27 and 6:11-12 as the one who seeks to disrupt the relationships within the church and the one against whom our battle is ultimately to be fought. The air is the 'intermediate sphere between earth and heaven'[2] and in that sense is another way of describing the abode of the principalities and powers,

---

2   O'Brien, *Ephesians*, p. 160.

against whom our battle is to be fought and over whom Jesus has all authority.

It is a great comfort to know that when the Lord returns we will both see and experience his total victory in the domain of Satan, for at his return the 'dead in Christ will rise first. After that we who are still alive and are left will be caught up together with them in the clouds to meet the Lord in the air. And so we will be with the Lord forever.' (1 Thess. 4:16b-17). Paul's point here is not meteorological; rather, he is reminding his readers that those who trust Jesus will be with him when he appears. When the 'Son of Man comes in clouds with great power and glory' (Mark 13:26) those who are waiting for him will be gathered to him – in those very clouds. He is to return 'in the same way you have seen him go into heaven' (Acts 1:11b), namely, in a cloud. And as he returns and ushers in the resurrection and the new heaven and the new earth, the full manifestation of his glory will be experienced by those who belong to him.

Equally, just as we will experience the very presence of God in Christ in the material reality of the new heaven and new earth, so too the abode of Satan will be finally and fully vanquished when Jesus returns. The cycles of judgement in the book of Revelation, each of which presents an increasingly clear picture of what God will do before the Lord returns, remind us that when the seventh angel pours out the seventh bowl of God's wrath, it is poured 'into the air.' That is, into the realm of Satan. Only then, when Satan is finally destroyed, do we hear 'a loud voice from the throne saying "it is done."' (Rev. 16:17)

These references remind us that the 'air' is the realm in which Satan operates and which will one day be filled with the fullness of the victorious Jesus. In the book of

Ephesians, Paul needs to make it very clear that all people find themselves under his authority, living his way. He is at work in 'those who are disobedient' (literally 'the sons of disobedience'). This does not mean that everyone is demon-possessed, but it does mean that everyone serves this master, that although our actions outside of Christ may be thought to be free and personal, they are in fact directed away from God by Satan. All humanity serves one of two masters – the Lord Jesus or the Ruler of the Kingdom of the air.

When it comes to preaching this passage we will need to be sensitive to the fact that many of our hearers may not be aware of what the New Testament tells us about the realm or the activity of Satan. It can be rather unsettling to hear that without Christ we are under Satan's authority and it does not look as if those we know who do not follow Jesus belong to the devil.

It may be worth bearing in mind both the 'big picture' of scriptural revelation and the specific situation which confronted the church in Ephesus and of which all Christians need to be aware. The story of salvation history reminds us that humanity as a whole opted to move under Satan's authority in the Garden of Eden. 'Sin entered the world through one man . . . consequently . . . the result of one trespass was condemnation for all men.' (Rom. 5:12, 18) The actions of Genesis 3 left us spiritually dead, blind and serving the wrong master. In the sustaining goodness of God he has given us laws and society in order to minimalise the effect of sin and deal with those who are deemed to go beyond the bounds of accepted convention. But history also reminds how easy it is for those who regard themselves as decent and law-abiding to be exposed as evil, simply by changing the social or political framework in which they operate. The political regime in Germany in the 1930s, the civil wars in East Africa and in the Balkans are chilling examples of the evil which is latent in the human heart.

It may also be helpful to remind our hearers of the words of Jesus, which sum up the paradox of our experience: 'if you then, though you are evil, know how to give good gifts to your children ...' (Luke 11:13). Very few people do not want to give good gifts to their children, but when placed in a different context we discover that the evil of our hearts will bubble out into hatred, jealousy and bitterness.

When we turn from the big picture of humanity as presented in the Bible and experienced in history to the context of Ephesians, it is helpful to remember that those to whom Paul was writing were 'normal' citizens in proconsular Asia. Like most of us, those who met in the lecture hall of Tyrannus, those Jews who believed, and even those who practised sorcery would not have been regarded by others as particularly 'evil'. But as they were confronted with the truth and power of the gospel many came openly and confessed their evil deeds (Acts 19:18). The true state of their hearts was not exposed by a comparison with others around them but when confronted by the truth and power of the gospel.

In Ephesians, Paul is reminding the Christians of what they *were*, something they would have known only too well having experienced the redeeming truth and power of the gospel. So whilst it may be difficult for the world to see that it is under the authority of Satan (indeed, the fact that he has blinded the mind of unbelievers means that they will not see), it is not difficult for those who have had their eyes opened and been rescued by Christ. To that end our preaching must understand both the 'big picture' of God's rescue (and the spiritual need for it) as well as the personal experience of those Christians to whom we are speaking. If non-Christians are present, as happens week by week in many of our churches, wisdom and sensitivity will be required – but it is not that difficult to convince most people that their sin is serious and that they can do nothing about it, that the master they follow is not the God who made us or the Saviour who rescued us. Once we have moved the means of assessment from our position in relation to others to our position in relation to God (the one who sees and knows everything we have thought, said or done, publicly and privately), sin, evil and the reality of another master become more evident.

The *cravings of our sinful nature or passions of the flesh* are far more than the carnal excesses associated with lust or gluttony. It is not only our bodies that are influenced by trespasses and sins; it is also our minds. The full nature of these appetites can be appreciated by reading through Ephesians and noting down the opposite of all instructions which relate to walking God's ways. Chapters 4, 5 and 6 are packed with descriptions of what this new life looks like, *created to be like God in true righteousness and holiness* (4:24). When we fail to walk his ways but walk the way of the world, all these God-given qualities find their opposites. Such are the cravings of the flesh.

We were condemned

The resulting condition of humanity without Christ is that we were *by nature objects of wrath*. God's holy anger against sin is directed to those who by nature are sinful. Humanity has no hope outside Christ.

The doctrine of God's wrath is unpopular in modern culture, both within and outside the church. We want a loving and forgiving God who will deal with us in ways which give us the assurance that all will be well. We find it difficult to think of a God who might be angry with his creation, even if his anger is righteous and not tainted by sinful motives. But when we pause and think about it, none of us operates in the way we want God to behave. When we see injustice, particularly when experienced personally, we cry out. We want perpetrators to be caught and justice to be done. We do not like the thought of wrongdoing being unpunished; unless, of course, it is we who have committed the offence.

If God were to behave in such ways, there would be no justice. God would either have to forgive those we thought should be brought to justice or he would have to set an artificial barrier so that all those who had committed offences no worse than our own would be accepted by him whilst those we deem as unacceptable – the murderer, the rapist, the paedophile – would be excluded. But what if the murderer could explain the extraordinary circumstances that brought about his actions? Would he be inclined to make a special case? And what if we discovered someone else, in slightly different circumstances, who could make an equally valid case? For justice to be done on those terms we would have to become both judge and jury. But then who would decide what is acceptable and what is not when cultures and codes vary across the world?

The trouble with our view of justice is that it is tainted by the very mindset described in Ephesians 2:1-3. We would be far better to have a perfect judge, untainted by sins, with perfect standards, whose judgement was both absolute and trustworthy. Our problem is that when we find such a judge, his verdict on us is 'guilty.' We fall far short of the perfection required. Like the rest, we were by nature objects of wrath.

What God has done – The power of love (2:4-7)

Verses 1-3 are fundamental to our understanding of verses 4-7. For without a correct diagnosis of humanity we will not grasp the wonder and magnitude of God's love and grace. Here we come to the heart of this passage with its main subject – God – and its main verb – to make alive.

> But because of his great love for us, God, who is rich in mercy, made us alive with Christ even when we were dead in transgressions – it is by grace that you have been saved. And God raised us up with Christ and seated us with him in the heavenly realms in Christ Jesus, in order that in the coming ages he might show the incomparable riches of his grace, expressed in his kindness to us in Christ Jesus.

The motivation for God's action lies in his character alone. He has great love for those who are the objects of his wrath, who walk in ways entirely contrary to what he desires and what he has purposed for humanity. He is rich in mercy, and those incomparable riches are seen and expressed in the Lord Jesus Christ.

Remember that this section flows from the prayer which we read at the end of Chapter 1. God has raised Jesus to life and seated him in the heavenly realms, far above all rule and authority, power and dominion and every title that can be given, not only in the present age but in the one to come.

What is quite extraordinary is that, having made it clear that we are dead and incapable therefore of change, God has done for us spiritually what he did for Christ physically. Christ was raised from death to life; so are we. Christ was seated in the heavenly realms; so are we. The destiny and privilege experienced by Christ alone has been made ours by the grace, mercy and love of God.

Our present spiritual location is of the utmost importance for our understanding of what it means to be the church. Paul has explained the extent of our spiritual blessings in Christ, which are to be found in the heavenly realms. He has prayed for the Ephesians that they might know the power of God, which has been seen and expressed in raising Jesus from death to those heavenly realms. And now God has done the same for the believer. That power is available because it has been demonstrated and experienced. What is more, the place in which we now find ourselves (spiritually speaking) is with Christ, far above all rule and authority. He has been placed there for the church, for us; and we now find ourselves receiving all the benefits of being there with him, the benefits already introduced to us in 1:3-14.

Not only has God rescued us from one master – the ruler of the kingdom of the air – but he has placed our identity firmly with another – the Lord Jesus Christ. And his rule is far superior. He has authority and dominion over Satan.

It means that when we read of Satan's activity in disturbing the relationships within the church (4:27) and we read of the battle to be the church in chapter 6, all that is necessary for that battle to be won and for the church to live as the church has already been achieved in Christ and in the heavenly realms. It is from the security of our identity – who we are – that we are able to become who we are in our day to day living.

Paul wants us to be very clear about what God has done and where we now belong, so that we can live as God's people now while we wait for the full experience of what has been won for us in Christ. Throughout history and for all eternity the existence of a rescued and reconciled people, the church, is an expression of *'the incomparable riches of God's grace, expressed in his kindness to us in Christ Jesus'*. God displays his goodness in creating the church.

The walk of grace (2:8-10)

Grace is such an alien concept to our distorted minds that Paul includes two negatives as he summarises the effect of God's grace on those who receive it.

The first negative is that our grace-driven salvation, which is appropriated by faith, is not from ourselves but is a gift from God. It is all too easy to think of faith as something we offer to God in order to take hold of what he wants to give us. But if that were the case, then Paul's initial diagnosis would be incorrect. Dead people cannot take hold of anything. If faith is dependent on us, then we are not really dead in sin; we would be capable of making a decision for or against God. The reality is more serious. We cannot make decisions for ourselves. We may appear to choose God, but that is only because he chose us before the foundation of the world. It is all by grace, even the faith by which we take hold of his promises. It is his gift to us. Our salvation and the faith by which we are included in Christ are all from him.

Whilst not all commentators would hold that faith itself is included in the gift of faith and whilst this never diminishes the human element of coming to faith and proclaiming the faith, we must nevertheless remember that it is God who builds his church through the Lord Jesus. He will not lose any of those God has given to him, but raise them up on the last day (John 6:39). It is deeply humbling that all our salvation is from him. We deserve nothing but condemnation, yet he has made us his children.

The second negative follows on from this – our grace-driven salvation is not by works. There is no human performance which can generate approval or acceptance with God. We have nothing to offer. We cannot boast in anything we have done for him, for there is nothing God needs or wants. He loved us despite the fact that we were rebels against him. Even our on-going Christian living is dependent on his grace and initiative.

Many Christians are taught that the Christian life is a life of loving response to God's goodness and kindness. God has graciously rescued us in the Lord Jesus Christ: now what can we do for him? But such teaching is to misunderstand grace. It would be like a parent saying to his teenage son, 'look at all I have done for you. What will you give me in return?' No, our good works are not in response to God's gracious initiative, but are part of it. The true Christian is seen by good works – such is the walk to which we have been called in Christ - but he knows that those works are totally grace driven, prepared in advance. There is nothing we have and nothing we offer to merit salvation or approval. Those who walk in his ways do so because of his grace. It is, or should be, the way the church walks, for we are *God's* workmanship. As John Newton's famous hymn puts it:

> Twas grace that taught my heart to fear
> And grace my fears relieved;
> How precious did that grace appear,
> The hour I first believed!
>
> Through many dangers, toils and snares
> I have already come
> Tis grace has brought me safe thus far
> And grace will lead me home.

From text to teaching

The danger of a passage like Ephesians 2:1-10 is that, in many ways, we think we know it too well. It contains glorious gospel truths; the best 'but' in the Bible, as it was once described. But we face the same danger of taking the passage in isolation from what precedes and follows it. The direction of Paul's thinking is that we might understand what God has done to make us a people, both in the heavenly realms and then in the church's manifestation on earth. Although we come to God through Christ as individuals, we are called to be a people. We must not reduce this to the level simply of 'my salvation', for if we do, we may learn great and true doctrines, but we will not fully understand Ephesians, and we will not be transformed into the picture of God's future purposes that he longs us to be.

It may be useful to pick up the language of 'walking.' We all used to walk one way; by grace we are now able to walk another. One is the walk of death, the other the walk of life. In addition, we need to make it clear that by grace we have been raised to that place where Christ now is, and that the power which placed him there (and which is available to us) has already been experienced by us in making us into God's new people.

Preaching outline – an example

The sermon titles suggested below are rather bare and, without careful planning or more creative wording, they may not serve to anchor the extraordinary content of the passage. We need to convey both the majesty and depth of what Paul is teaching and its connection with what precedes it (Paul's prayer) and what he will go on to teach. Whilst the challenge for how we live out these truths will be made in the application, the introduction must serve to surprise the Christian. The link between 1:23 and 2:1 is not what we would expect. Having had a wonderful description of the church (his body, the fullness of him who fills everything in every way 1:23) we now have the apostolic finger pointed at Gentile Christians 'as for you, you were dead' (2:1). Without the self-realisation of the divine diagnosis of our condition, grace becomes disempowered. That is the reason for which Paul writes and which we need to tap into for our sermons to have power.

1. The walk of death (2:1-3)

2. The power of love (2:4-7)

3. The walk of grace (2:8-10)

Application

This is a rich passage. The application of what it means to be without Christ must be made, but will, for many, be challenging. Paul's inclusion of himself is helpful here, as is the place of the passage in the letter. He is writing to Christians, those who have been saved, so that they might realise, perhaps for the first time, what that salvation involved. This is not an evangelistic passage. It is a passage for the church. We need to grasp the love and grace of God, which ripped us from condemnation and raised us with Christ, if we are to live as God wants us to live.

The consequence of who we are is not that we must live our lives in loving response (although there is some truth in this) but rather that the life of love is the natural and expected out-working of what God has done, by grace. The new walk is the sign of new life. Here we can make many links with the congregation. If we are not walking in this way (which will be explained further in chapters 4-6 of the letter) the question of whether we have grasped the gospel or responded to the gospel can legitimately be raised. Those who have been rescued walk a different way.

Questions for home groups/study groups

Familiar passages are particularly challenging for the small group leader. It can be difficult for those who have been Christians for a while to realise that this was written to believers in order that we might be able to be what God has made us to be. We want to marvel at what God has done; but equally we want to be challenged by the contrast between the old walk and the new. The application of this passage is seen in the lives of those who study it, both individually and corporately. It can never be detached from the rest of the letter, which constantly challenges us to be the people we have been made to be by virtue of being raised with Christ.

We may also find ourselves sidetracked by the question of people's experience of new birth. The Bible is very clear that people come to Christ because they heard the gospel. There is persuasion, proclamation and prayer. A brief reading of Paul's missionary journey to Ephesus will show that new life was hard won. People then, as now, need to hear and be challenged. Sometimes the process of coming to Christ takes several years. But behind our experience is the spiritual reality of verses 1-3. That is what Paul wants his readers to understand, in order that they might better grasp what God has done to make the church, and why that is so important. Special care will be needed so that we might maintain that same focus in a small group.

Suggested Questions

1. How is humanity described in 2:1-3? In what way does this description surprise you?

2. What has God done about this condition? Why has he done it?

3. What is the effect for the believer?

4. Explain how what has happened physically to Jesus is mirrored spiritually in the believer.

5. How is this salvation seen in the life of the believer?

6. From our studies of Ephesians so far, what spiritual certainties does the believer have in the past, in the present and in the future?

4

A MAMMOTH TASK II (2:11-22)

We have two great disadvantages when we come to read the Bible, and particularly when we come to texts such as Ephesians 2:11-22. The first is that we fail to grasp the significance of God's eternal purposes. Our thinking has been so shaped by the mindset of our age (particularly over the last 200 years) that we have diminished salvation to what happens to 'me' and we have de-materialised the promise of God for the future. 'Heaven' becomes a loose notion of disembodied spirits and 'salvation' becomes some vague concept of what enables me to become one of them. But God's purposes relate to a New Heaven and New Earth where he will be with a transformed people. His purposes are heading to that day when 'all things in heaven and earth are brought together under one head, even Christ.' The formation of a new people is at the heart of his eternal purposes.

The second disadvantage we have is that we fail to see just how far from those purposes we are without Christ. Paul has spent the first part of chapter two making it clear what God has had to do in Christ to rescue us, Jew and Gentile. This rescue is so that we can be the people he wants us to be, walking paths he has fore-ordained, so that we might become a picture to the world of what God will do in all history. We will be a picture to the rulers and authorities in the heavenly realms of his extraordinary wisdom and grace. Now he wants to make it clear what we in particular were (as Gentile people) prior to this gospel grace exploding into our lives.

Preliminary observations

Paul uses the same schema in the second half of the chapter as he did in the first, namely 'what you were' and 'what you are.' If the first part of the chapter related primarily to our relationship with God (the 'vertical dimension' of salvation), the second half relates primarily to our relationship with one another (the 'horizontal dimension'). Both these reconciliations relate entirely to the work of Christ and result in a radically new people, the church. As Paul concludes the chapter, it is therefore a description of the church which is presented, a picture which will be explained more fully in the second half of the book as we discover how that which has been created in Christ can become a reality in our local churches.

Listening to the text

(11) Therefore, remember that formerly you who are Gentiles by birth and called 'uncircumcised' by those who call themselves 'the circumcision' (that done in the body by the hands of men) – (12) remember that at that time you were separate from Christ, excluded from citizenship in Israel and foreigners to the covenants of the promise,

without hope and without God in the world. (13) But now in Christ Jesus you who once were far away have been brought near through the blood of Christ. (14) For he himself is our peace, who has made the two one and has destroyed the barrier, the dividing wall of hostility, (15) by abolishing in his flesh the law with its commandments and regulations. His purpose was to create in himself one new man out of the two, thus making peace (16) and in this one body to reconcile both of them to God through the cross, by which he put to death their hostility. (17) He came and preached peace to you who were far away and peace to those who were near. (18) For through him we both have access to the Father by one Spirit. (19) Consequently, you are no longer foreigners and aliens, but fellow-citizens with God's people and members of God's household, (20) built on the foundation of the apostles and prophets, with Christ Jesus himself as the chief cornerstone. (21) In him the whole building is joined together and rises to become a holy temple in the Lord. (22) And in him you too are being built together to become a dwelling in which God lives by his Spirit.

The text divides naturally into three main sections:

1. 2:11-13   What we were without Christ

2. 2:14-18   What Christ did to make the church

3. 2:19-22   What the church looks like

What we were without Christ (2:11-13)

Chapter 2:11-22 is linked to the previous section by the word 'therefore.' The reconciliation of sinners to the creator God through the Lord Jesus cannot be separated from what it means to be the church. Indeed, Paul links the one directly with the other with the word 'therefore.' He wants them to remember what they were so that they can understand what they are.

The particular focus of this 'remembering' is that those of us who are Gentiles 'in the flesh' (not 'by birth' as in the NIV) were, in that state, utterly separated from God. The emphasis on the flesh highlights the very real, physical separation that existed between Jew and Gentile. Circumcision was a badge of the covenant, an outward sign of being a part of God's people – and yet he is clear to point out that it was only 'in the flesh.' It was external, human, done 'by the hands of men' and not by God.

Nevertheless, the separation was real. The Jew-Gentile division was one of the most 'fundamental divisions in the first century world.'[1] In his commentary on the letter John Stott quotes from Barclay:

> The Jew had an immense contempt for the Gentile. The Gentiles, said the Jews, were created by God to be fuel for the fires of hell. God, they said, loves only Israel of all the nations he had made ... it was not even lawful to render help to a Gentile mother in her hour of sorest need, for that would simply be to bring another Gentile into the world. Until Christ came, the Gentiles were an object of contempt to the Jews. The barrier between them was absolute. If a Jewish boy married a Gentile girl, or if a Jewish girl married a Gentile boy, the funeral of that Jewish boy or girl would be carried out. Such a contract with a Gentile was the equivalent of death.[2]

Paul wants the Ephesians to remember what they were by understanding the five serious deficiencies of the Gentile state.

---

1   O'Brien, *Ephesians*, p. 194.
2   Stott, *Ephesians*, p. 91.

First, they were 'separate from Christ'. The expectation of a Messiah was a Jewish expectation. Even though the Old Testament increasingly makes reference to the one who would be a light for the Gentiles, the Messiah was not promised to them. The anointed king, the Christ, was not a Gentile hope.

Second, they were separated from 'citizenship in Israel'. This is better translated 'from the commonwealth of Israel'. Gentiles were excluded from the people of God. The benefits and promises which were given exclusively to God's Old Testament people were not open to those who were not part of his covenant community.

Third, the Gentiles were therefore 'foreigners to the covenants'. The plural 'covenants' indicates not only the foundational covenant to Abraham, but also the Mosaic covenant and the Davidic covenant, in which God promised the eternal 'Christ'.

The fourth and fifth deficiencies are the result of this exclusion. Gentiles – you and me if we are not Jews – were 'without hope and without God'.

Of course, the revealed mystery of the gospel, the shock of the gospel, which was not made known in previous generations as it has now been made known to God's holy apostles and prophets (3:5f) is that the Gentiles can now be included into the purposes of God and so become part of the new people of God. But prior to that revelation, Paul wanted his readers to be absolutely clear – and to remember – that they were in a desperate state.

And he wanted them to remember, so that they could understand the power of the gospel to make a new people. Hence verse 13 'but now . . .' The language picks up the fairly typical proselyte language of the Old Testament (e.g.

Isa. 57:19) which was used of people who became a part
of the Old Testament people of God. But here something
new is happening. God is not simply now adding Gentiles,
those who were alienated and without hope, to an already
established people; he is forming a new people in the Lord
Jesus Christ.

What Christ did to make the church (2:14-18)

Once again, the 'you' language becomes 'we' and 'our'. Those
alienated and those who possessed the covenants and the
promises alike are now made into one new man through
Jesus who is 'our peace'. We often talk of peace as that which
is created between two people; and those who are bringers
of peace are those who are able to negotiate and arbitrate
between warring factions. Here, however, something bigger
is going on, something new. Christ himself is the peace; he
is the place where this new entity is to be found. In him
we have the wisdom and understanding to realise that we
have every spiritual blessing in the heavenly realm. He does
not simply reconcile warring factions, he re-creates a new
humanity which is in itself a picture of God's purposes for
all eternity.

As a concept, 'peace' in the Old Testament, relates
to 'wholeness, particularly with reference to personal
relationships.'[3] Such wholeness by virtue of the creation of
a 'new man', a new humanity, is now possible.

The way in which that is brought about is explained in
verses 14-15. Jesus has destroyed the barrier ... '*by abolishing
in his flesh the law with its commandments and regulations*'.
Many read this with direct reference to the temple and to the
clear barrier of exclusion between the Court of the Gentiles
and the rest of the temple. On this barrier signs were

3   O'Brien, *Ephesians*, p. 193.

placed, written in Greek and Latin, reminding the Gentiles that they proceed on the pain of death. However, when we consider that the letter was written to people who may never have travelled to Jerusalem and for whom the imagery of the temple, important though it is for understanding this section of the letter, would have probably meant little, we need to consider whether Paul might have had another barrier in mind, of which the temple was only a symptom.

The real barrier was the Mosaic Law. That was the dividing wall of hostility, abolished; and destroyed through the death of Jesus. It is perhaps worth noting that just as Paul encouraged the Gentiles to remember their former state (Gentiles 'in the flesh') so now he reminds them that Jesus removed the barrier 'in his flesh.' The flesh of Jesus therefore removes all man-made barriers, created 'by the hands of men' that we might care to construct. The result of the cross is therefore a new people. It is not simply that a barrier was removed, so that those who had been excluded were included but something more profound – a new 'body' reconciled to God through the cross (v. 16).

It is important to realise that Paul knew all too well that law could not save. His argument here is not about the value or place of the law. It is, rather, how God works out his ultimate purposes. For although the Gentiles were excluded from all those Old Testament promises, the revelation of the gospel had shown Paul that Jew and Gentile were in the same boat – which is why he was able to say 'like the rest, we were by nature objects of wrath.' The Jews, as well as the Gentiles, needed the blood of Christ, not simply to reconcile individuals or people-groups to Christ, but to form a new people, the church. More than that, he also knew that 'what the law was powerless to do in that it was weakened by the sinful nature, God did by sending his own Son in the likeness of sinful man' (Rom. 8:3). In that sense, the law-promises given to the people of God, from which the Gentiles were excluded, have now found their fulfilment and completion (Rom. 10:4). The gospel shock is that, in that completion, the Messiah to whom they point created a new people out of those who had not received the law and were alienated from God's people.

And so, through the gospel, peace was and is preached. Now Jew and Gentile, in a new entity, can approach God with a confidence hitherto impossible and only made known in the gospel. God is in the business of constituting a new people, a people who will manifest the wisdom of God to the rulers and authorities in the heavenly realms (3:10) and a people who will be a picture of what God is doing in history (1:9-10). Now 'Jew and Gentile stand together as one people in God's presence with old distinctions no longer having significance.'[4]

What the church looks like (2:19-22)

The result of this unmerited grace-action on the part of God is a new people, pictured in these verses in three distinct but complementary ways. In the political realm the Gentiles are now part of God's people. In the domestic realm they are part of a new family; and in the spiritual realm, they are part of a new temple, the very place where God dwells by his Spirit.

Several characteristics of the church emerge here, each of which is developed later on in the letter. In the first place, the church is built on the foundation of the apostles and prophets. These are the ones to whom the risen Christ has made known the mystery of the gospel (3:5, 6; 4:11a). It

---

4   G.D. Fee, *God's Empowering Presence: The Holy Spirit in the Letters of Paul* (Peabody, USA: Hendrickson, 1994) p. 683.

means that the very content of the Gospel which Paul is explaining within this letter – a gospel which creates God's new humanity – has been given to them. It is, therefore, unlikely that Paul is referring to Old Testament prophets and New Testament apostles. Rather, the gospel message which creates the church and which was not made known to men in other generations (3:5) has now been revealed. These 'apostles and prophets' are a unique group of individuals whose teaching now constitutes what we have in the New Testament. Indeed, the documents in the New Testament were collated on the basis that each bore the apostolic badge of authenticity. It is their teaching which the church is called upon to preserve, proclaim and obey. Without their teaching, God's new humanity has no foundation.

Secondly, Jesus Christ is the chief cornerstone. This has echoes of Psalm 118:22 which is picked up by Jesus in Mark 12:10 and by Peter in 1 Peter 2:7. The chief cornerstone not only held the position of honour in a building, but was also fundamental for the building's efficacy. Without it the building could not be stable and could not therefore be extended and developed. It was fundamental to the integrity of the building in the same way that Jesus is fundamental to the integrity of the church: 'In him the whole building is joined together and rises to become a holy temple in the Lord.' (2:21) Paul is reminding us that the church is intimately related to and dependent upon the Lord Jesus Christ.

Thirdly, the church grows as those who have been rescued by his grace (both Jew and Gentile) are built together in him. The new humanity which he creates is fundamentally linked to Jesus. He is our 'head' and we are 'his body, the fullness of him who fills everything in every way.' (1:23). All our spiritual identity and blessings are to be found in him; we are his inheritance (1:14). What is more, the church is indwelt by his Spirit. The place in which God dwells is not the Temple in Jerusalem (nor, indeed, the pagan equivalent of the Artemis Temple in Ephesus) but in Jew and Gentile brought together by the blood of Jesus; or for us, in the local body of believers.

The church is pictured here as a dynamic, growing, organic body and although we have yet to discover how it grows and exactly what it looks like in action (something which we will see in the coming chapters), we have been presented with a powerful picture of this new humanity. Those who were dead and alienated both from God and from one another have been made into a radically new people through Jesus Christ, driven by his grace and love. He is fundamental to everything; without him there is no church. But the first layer of bricks, on which the whole church is built are those who hold the teaching given by the risen Jesus himself, a teaching preserved for us in the pages of the New Testament.

The miracle which brings this about is embodied in the content of these few verses. From the 'remember you' of verse 11 to the 'consequently you' of verse 19 something miraculous has happened, through the gospel, by the grace of God, creating a people which the world could not create, a picture of the end-time purposes of God. If only we could grasp what it means to have been rescued by this grace and made a part of this people!

From text to teaching

It seems wise to follow the natural flow of this passage when constructing a sermon series. Some may be tempted to take the second half of the chapter along with the first and in one sermon to look at the double reconciliation which is required to make God's new people; and whilst it can be very helpful to see that big sweep of God's saving purposes, (especially when we consider that Paul is writing to emphasise the significance of the church), there is potentially so much in this chapter that it might be wiser to break it into two sermons.

Either way, it is essential that the conclusion of 2:19-22 is not lost. Verses 19-22 are Paul's application of the truth he is unpacking in the preceding verses. We will not fully understand the significance of what it means to be church unless we understand the hopelessness of our situation without Christ and the power of God which was and is required to form a new people.

Introduction

As most of us become Christians and become members of churches without thinking very much about our Gentile background or the significance of the church, careful thought will need to be given to the 'hook' employed to pull people into the passage.

Many of us will be acutely aware of the alienations that divide people today: the tribal, national and religious divisions which have generated the wars and genocides of the last century (in East Africa, the Balkans, Northern Ireland, Central Europe, Communist Russia, Cambodia and the Middle East) are global examples of what we experience in the more domestic sphere of our own lives. Neighbours fall out, communication breaks down between husband and wife, parent and child, even within our churches. But as we preach this passage, we need to help our congregations to understand that *we* were alienated from God in just the

same way, and that we have absolutely no natural right to
approach him with the familiarity to which we have become
accustomed. As Gentile believers, we were on the outside;
we had no place in the covenant community of God. Our
only hope and the only way in which we can approach God
and become part of his people is by his unmerited grace
and love. We perhaps also need to think about the ministry
and mission of God's people today, especially where the
Old Testament and the Jewish nation are either forgotten
or viewed through theologically doubtful spectacles. What
does it mean today to be made a part of the Jew-Gentile
'new man'?

Preaching outline – an example

1. You were without hope   2:11-13

2. The miracle of the church   2:14-18

3. Church – do we look like this?   2:19-22

The first point in this outline needs to make the powerful
point that we were in an utterly hopeless position. The
strength of the language in 2:12-13 hammers the nail of
exclusion firmly into our minds. We had no part of God's
people and as such we need to convey the total desperation
of our situation, which will not automatically be felt in
many of our rather comfortable churches. Once again, there
needs to be something of a shock factor in the first point.
Paul is taking his readers back to the situation before they
received the blessings of 1:1-14. We need to do the same.

Once we have established what life was like before we
came to Christ we can then begin to teach what Christ has
done, but note that Paul's focus is on the church: our peace,
the two having become one, the barrier destroyed, the law

abolished (achieved 'in his flesh' and 'in himself'). Only then does he focus on the fact that this new man is reconciled to God (through the cross). We are not only presented with a very high theology of the church but also the stark reality that without being a part of this people we have no access to the Father. Our natural thinking tends to reverse these two truths: we will tend to be more individualistic and have a relatively low view of the church and many of us will think that our position before God (and access to him) is not related to being a part of the people he has made. In speaking of the miracle of the church we might also include something of the shock and significance of the church. We will certainly need to be aware that most of us do not think like Paul. We need to have our thinking changed.

Although the third point above is written as a question, the text is more of a statement of what the church is. It naturally follows the first two sections, reminding us of what we were before becoming part of the church and what we now are as part of the church. Once that has been established we can begin to think about what this looks like; in other words, what will be true of all those who have been rescued by Christ and made a part of his new people. The place of the Bible, the centrality of Jesus and the organic, Spirit-filled nature of the church will give much food for thought.

Application

The application of this passage lies in Paul's conclusion. We will need to do some work to help people to realise our plight without Christ, and the fact that the church is a new Jew-Gentile entity of which we are enormously privileged to be a part. The significance that we are no longer foreigners and aliens but fellow-citizens with God's people and members of God's household is of profound importance. It helps us to have a right understanding of the significance of the church in the purposes of God and of how the gospel works to create it.

Equally, our application must focus on Paul's description of the church. Verses 20-22 provide a stunning summary of the dynamic nature of the church, what it is built upon and who is at its centre. This powerful picture, unpacked in subsequent chapters, is a long way from the consumer-driven, individualistic mindset so prevalent in the 21st century church.

Questions for home groups/study groups

Most of us have rather distorted ideas of what it means to be church, learned in the subcultures of our own particular churches. The challenge of what it means to be church which arises from these verses may not be expected and the implications of what we find may result in some heart-searching questions.

Suggested questions

1. How would you define the church? What features would you say are fundamental to the people of God and which are merely cultural preference?

2. What does Paul want his Gentile readers to remember? Why might this be?

3. What is the effect of the 'blood of Christ' (v. 13)?

4. According to these words, what was the purpose of the death of Jesus?

5. What did Jesus abolish? Why might this be of particular significance to the Gentiles who received this letter?

6. Summarise Paul's description of the church (vv. 19-22). What does it mean to be built on the foundation of the apostles and prophets (see 3:5; 4:11)?

7. How is the church related to God the Father, God the Son and God the Holy Spirit?

8. How does this description of church differ from the answer you gave to the first question above?

9. Where do you need to change in your thinking and in your behaviour?

5

HOW IMPORTANT IS THE CHURCH?
(3:1-13)

It may seem rather strange to entitle this section of the letter 'how important is the church?' but as Paul begins this chapter his autobiographical interlude is linked directly with what we have just read about the church in 2:19-22. It is so important that we, as Gentiles, understand the significance of what it means to become a part of this new humanity that, although he is about to pray for the church (the words 'for this reason' are picked up again in 3:14), Paul breaks off to explain how he came to understand it this way himself. His claims are so significant that we need to be sure they are of God; how else would we have the courage to say that the church is an outcrop of eternity, a picture of what God will one day do in fullness when the times have reached their fulfilment?

Preliminary observations
Although this appears to be no more than an autobiographical interlude, these words help us to understand the foundation of the church (2:20) and how the church

is going to grow into what she already is (4:11). It is also important for us, who do not usually consider these things, to realise that the revealed mystery of the gospel is not simply about my salvation but about the formation of a new people of God. Apart from verse 1 and the single sentence in verse 13, the passage breaks naturally into two sections: verses 2-7 which explain how the grace of God gave Paul this message and ministry, and verses 8-12 which explain how the grace of God empowered Paul for this ministry. Once understood we can begin to see how significant this is for our understanding of the church and how the church relates to the world and the cosmos.

Listening to the text

(1) For this reason I, Paul, the prisoner of Christ Jesus for the sake of you Gentiles— (2) Surely you have heard about the administration of God's grace that was given to me for you, (3) that is, the mystery made known to me by revelation, as I have already written briefly. (4) In reading this, then, you will be able to understand my insight into the mystery of Christ, (5) which was not made known to men in other generations as it has now been revealed to God's holy apostles and prophets. (6) This mystery is that through the gospel the Gentiles are heirs together with Israel, members together of one body, and sharers together in the promise in Christ Jesus. (7) I became a servant of this gospel by the gift of God's grace given me through the working of his power. (8) Although I am less than the least of all God's people, this grace was given me: to preach to the Gentiles the unsearchable riches of Christ, (9) and to make plain to everyone the administration of this mystery, which for ages past was kept hidden in God, who created all things. (10) His intent was that

now, through the church, the manifold wisdom of God
should be made known to the rulers and authorities in
the heavenly realms, (11) according to his eternal purpose
which he accomplished in Christ Jesus our Lord. (12) In
him and through faith in him we may approach God with
freedom and confidence. (13) I ask you, therefore, not to
be discouraged because of my sufferings for you, which
are your glory.

Paul could not have known anything about this gospel had
it not been revealed to him by the grace of God (vv. 2-3). He
was a pious, religious Jew with a deep working knowledge
of the scriptures, but even with that knowledge the church-
forming gospel was not known to him. By that same grace
Paul was commissioned to proclaim that mystery to others
(vv. 7-8). So we have here *revelation* (from God to Paul) and
commission (the proclaiming of this truth). Only as Paul
fulfils his commission of proclaiming this revealed truth
can we become a part of the church and taste this irresistible
grace of God for ourselves.

The significance of the Gospel is highlighted in some
ways by Paul's own experience as the apostle to the Gentiles.
The formation and existence of the church, which has
dominated the second chapter of the letter, drives Paul to his
knees and to the prayer which will be the subject of our next
section. But before he breaks off into the autobiographical
fragment of verses 2-13, which precedes the prayer, we are
reminded (in v. 1) of what Paul personally experienced as
a result of his conviction and commitment to the message
of this letter. His arrest and subsequent imprisonments in
Jerusalem, Ceasarea and Rome were as a direct consequence
of his mission to the Gentiles. It was the message of the
grace-empowered gospel in which Jew and Gentile were

brought together as one without the necessity of the Jewish law which had resulted in the chains he now bore. Had he not been committed to bringing the gospel to the Gentiles, he would not have experienced such opposition at the hands of Jewish fanatics. That very mission 'for the sake of you Gentiles' is the mission of the Lord Jesus – and for that reason Paul knows that although in human terms he is held under the authority of Roman rule, his imprisonment is 'of (or for) Jesus Christ.'

This God-given commitment to the authentic Jew-Gentile gospel and the situation which resulted from it gives Paul cause to delay the explanation of his prayer in order that he might elaborate his unique role given to him by God to bring the gospel to the Gentiles.

Revelation – the mystery revealed (3:2-7)

Paul assumes that his Gentile readers will have heard about his unique role as their apostle. This would perhaps suggest that some of them did not know him personally, but have only *heard* about his ministry, further strengthening the case that this letter might have been written for a wider audience than the church in Ephesus alone. The city's central role within proconsular Asia and the fact that from it all Asia heard the Word of the Lord (Acts 19:10) would make the clarification of Paul's unique role all the more important.

Verse 2 does just that. The word Paul uses relating to the 'administration' of God's grace (oikonomia) is applied elsewhere to God's ultimate grace purposes (1:10 NIV 'to be put into effect' but literally 'for a stewardship' and 3:9 ESV 'the plan of the mystery'). But here Paul connects the Word to his role in making the ultimate purposes of God known specifically to the Gentiles. God had revealed to Paul how the

Gentiles fit into his perfect purposes for the world; something previously hidden and now disclosed to the apostle.

In verses 3,4 and verse 6 Paul therefore speaks of a mystery which has been made known; a mystery previously hidden to men in other generations, but now revealed to God's holy apostles and prophets (v. 5). This mystery is 'that through the gospel the Gentiles are heirs together with Israel, members together of one body and sharers together in the promise in Christ Jesus.' (v. 6). God's purpose, hidden but now revealed, the mystery of Christ, is that God has created a church in Christ, made up of those who were alienated (Jew and Gentile) and now made into a new entity called 'the church'.

This revelation, which took place on the road to Damascus, turned Paul's life upside down. The revelation of Christ 'in him' (Gal. 1:12, 15-16) necessitated a radical re-thinking of what the Old Testament really meant and how it was fulfilled in Christ, the result of which was the gospel given to and preached by Paul. It went against his education, his training, his learning and everything he had previously based his life upon.

The wording clearly means his readers were able to access something of what he had previously written (v. 4). Some suggest this might be the letter to the Colossians, but without the certainty of knowing this, it might be wiser to assume that Paul is referring to the previous chapter(s), which when read out loud to the church or churches would make more sense of the phrase 'as I have already written briefly.' (NIV) They have just heard the extraordinary explanation of the formation of the new humanity, made up of Jew and Gentile reconciled in Christ; now they are told that this information came by the revelation of God to

Paul. His desire, and indeed his prayer (1:17) is that they and we might know that better.

Verse 7 ends this section by taking us back to the grace with which it began (v. 2). Paul became a servant (or 'minister') of the gospel by the gift of God's grace. This was no passive reception of information but rather an outworking of the power of God. It took the power of God to transform him from persecutor to saint and he still requires the power of God to enable him to do the ministry which has been entrusted to him. Such a 'power encounter' is a pre-requisite for all authentic conversion and all authentic Christian ministry of the people of God (1:19; 3:16, 18, 20; 6:10).

Commission – the mystery must be made known (3:8-13)

Having received the gospel by the grace of God, Paul then explains how that same grace has empowered and equipped him to preach this gospel to the nations. At no point does he elevate himself in this ministry; far from it, he refers to himself as the very least of all God's people. Grace alone propels him into the world with this gospel.

The word Paul uses in verse 8 for 'preach' is 'evangelise.' Paul has been telling Gentiles the good news, the unsearchable riches of Christ, spelled out in the first part of this letter, from 1:3. The good news is that those who were without Christ, without God and without hope in the world can be made into a new people, alive and raised with Christ; they can become the very place where God dwells; they can partake in the unsearchable riches of Christ.

The closest we can get to understanding the nature of these 'unsearchable riches' which Paul preaches is to meditate on the great eulogy of 1:3-14. Paul is seeking to make known what in some ways is greater than knowledge, all of which relates to the person and work of the Lord Jesus Christ (v. 8).

His grace-empowered responsibility is to bring to light what God has revealed to him which, once again, is the 'administration' of the revealed mystery. The word used in verse 9 is the same as that of 1:10 and 3:2. It is the ultimate plan of God to create a new people in Christ – not simply his rescue plan for a fallen world; but his ultimate plan before the foundation of the world (1:4, 5, 9, 10).

What was hidden is now public truth. And so, in 3:9 Paul writes about enlightening the world with this revealed mystery. He wants all people to hear about Christ and his creation of the church, the 'one man' of which he has been writing, centred on Christ and indwelt by the Spirit, so that through the church God's eternal purposes may be made known.

The implications of Paul's words are quite extraordinary. Paul wants the world to know that in the church God's future purposes for the world are to be seen. The church is the place where God is already drawing together those who are alienated. His eternal purposes (1:9-10) are now seen (or should be seen) in the 'new man' of the church.

As that happens, the rulers and authorities in the heavenly realms – that place above, where our battle to be church is fought and to which Jesus has been raised – recognise the very wisdom of God in operation. As the church lives as the church, the powers which stand opposed to us shudder, knowing their days are numbered. Before their eyes a picture of the future is emerging as those who previously were alienated in immovable hostility are now joined together in love and service. Such a miracle can only be achieved by the grace and wisdom of God, which as we already know, are to be found in Christ alone (cf. 1:7-8; 2:4). One day every knee will bow before the Lord Jesus, and the powers which oppose the church and seek to undermine the gospel will be no more. When that begins to happen in the church it is of such spiritual significance that it stirs the rulers and authorities in the heavenly realm to marvel at the manifold wisdom of God (v. 10).

Manifold is literally 'many coloured.' It was a word used of different coloured petals on plants. And in the same way members of this new humanity, the church, are many coloured: Jew and Gentile – or perhaps, in our context, those with different coloured skin, or of different social status – some poor, some wealthy, some educated, some uneducated. The power of the gospel is seen as people, who in the world would not give each other the time of day, are brought together with a new identity, centred on the Lord Jesus, indwelt by the Spirit. Such a people can never be created by man's effort but only by the irresistible grace of God.

It is both humbling and exhilarating to think that the local fellowships of believers, of which we are all a part, are pictures of what God is going to do in eternity. Until that day when the new heavens and earth are created and the visible unity God purposes is seen in its fullness and glory, the only visual point of contact between the heavenly realms and the earthly realms is the church. That is why church is so important and why church is so difficult. Satan does not want the church to be what we are – for when we live rightly, then it becomes apparent to Satan that his days are numbered, and to the world that the power and purposes of God are in operation. As we love one another and live as the church, the world sees that we are disciples and the principalities and powers get a foretaste of their future destruction.

The tangible point of reference for God's eternal purpose was seen in the Jew welcoming the Gentile into his house or in the marriage of a Christian girl of Jewish background to a Christian boy of Gentile background. In our day it might be seen when young and old talk as brothers, when the duke and the dustman relate to each other as valued friends, when black and white or rich and poor live in Christian harmony. When that happens, God's eternal purposes are being worked out (v. 11).

No wonder that Paul reminds the readers of the immensely privileged position which results from the gospel. We have unique privilege, both in relation to one another and in relation to God (v. 12).

This is the reason Paul gives for the Ephesians not to be worried about his present sufferings. His imprisonment may have been seen as a set-back for the gospel, but that very gospel, the very truth which has shaped the content of this letter, has put him there. It is for their benefit. It is as if, for Paul, the formation of the church is so important that nothing matters in comparison with the proclamation of this message to the world (v. 13).

From text to teaching

Church is far more important than many people realise. The local fellowships from which we come, the groups of people brought together by the gospel, are pictures of what God is doing in eternity and when they rightly live, they cause Satan to shudder. So although the world may look at us and say the church is irrelevant, a hangover from the past, redundant in modern society, the reality is that church is where history is heading, not a hangover from the past but a picture of the future. It is therefore of more relevance and importance than the countless projects which fill our minds and hearts so much of the time.

As we preach this passage, we will have choices to make. If we are preaching a series we may decide not to explain the significance of the apostles and prophets at this point. They have already come up in 2:20 and are fundamental to the argument of 4:1-16, which explains how we can become what we are. It may be that the shock of the gospel itself is enough.

Introduction

Many people are unaware why the church is important and indeed, how the message of the gospel relates to the formation of the church. With that in mind, an introduction which addresses the question 'how important is the church?' might take people to the very heart of this section. In order to do that it may be necessary to contrast Paul's situation with our own.

Paul was prepared to accept imprisonment in order that he might make the gospel clear; a gospel which unites previously warring factions in Christ. He was also aware that when that happens the rulers and authorities in the heavenly realms see the purposes of God and the wisdom of God being worked out in the day to day life of believers.

If our introduction can challenge the preconceptions of those to whom we are speaking, then we will have created the 'space' into which the sermon can be preached. We might ask the congregation 'is there anything for which you would be prepared to go to prison?' or 'what do you think unsettles Satan?' The answer to both those questions is 'the church' as described and explained by the words in this passage. As we proceed, we will need to take care to explain the fact (or remind people of the fact) that in Ephesians the real shock is that Gentiles can be a part of God's people. This was the 'mystery of Christ' hidden for long ages past but now revealed by God's grace to the apostles and prophets. For that to be understood and proclaimed, the power of God is required.

Preaching outline

The sermon outline suggested below seeks to challenge presuppositions with the first question and then to revisit the same question at the end of the sermon, in order to give the correct answer by way of application.

How important is the church?

1. The mystery   – grace revealed   3:2-7
2. The commission   – grace empowered   3:8-12

An alternative way of preaching the sermon might be to pick up both the shock of this revelation and the necessity of its proclamation:

+ The shock of revelation – you can be part of the church

+ The necessity of proclamation – the world must know this truth

+ The result

  + Satan will see God's wisdom

  + Sinners can approach God's throne

  + Suffering for the gospel makes sense

Application

Once again, Paul's application flows from the direction
of the passage. Paul's apostleship is crucial here and even
though it may not be dwelt upon at this stage, it is worth
noting that the gospel is for the world, both in the need for
it to be proclaimed and in the picture of the future which
results.

As the gospel takes root in the church the manifold
wisdom of God should be seen. It will not only be a statement
to the principalities and powers in the heavenly realms
(where our battle to be the church is to be fought) but will
also indicate the eternal purposes of God, accomplished
through the Lord Jesus Christ.

The very practical outworking of this should be seen in
the lives of those to whom we preach. It touches on how
we relate to one another, where we sit, who we talk to,
what we say after church. It takes the relationships within
the congregation on to a new level as we begin to realise
how significant they are as a picture of what God is doing.
Equally we may also begin to realise how damaging it can be
when we create barriers between Christian people, or refuse
to speak to someone because they happen to be different
from us, or harbour ill feelings towards someone rather
than forgive them, or elevate our preferences to the level of
theology. Whenever we insist that something about which
the Bible is silent should be done in a particular way and
that we will not partake unless it is, we are undermining the
gospel. If we insist on certain services, or songs, or liturgy
or clothing, neutral and harmless though they might be on
their own, we run the danger of weakening the church and
allowing the principalities and powers to mock rather than

marvel. When that which God has created is undermined, the cause of the gospel is knocked back and Satan, rather than shuddering, smiles.

Questions for home groups/study groups

In this passage we have one of the most significant sections in Ephesians. The statement of 3:10-11 is of profound importance for our understanding of what it means to be church and it must be seen in the light of the whole letter. The principalities and powers in the heavenly realms can so easily be misunderstood and the dynamic of a study group can lead to great confusion rather than clarity. The blessings which we have in heavenly realms are located in Christ but at the same time our battle to be the church is against the spiritual forces of evil in the heavenly realms. It is possible that many will have in mind an idea of equal contest and uncertain victory, but it must be remembered that the location of Christ is *above* all rule and authority, power and dominion. He has authority *over* the rulers in the heavenly realms. As those who been raised with Christ and seated with him live rightly now, in the church, the manifold wisdom of God is revealed, according to end time purposes of God (1:9-10).

The study group need not unpack all that Ephesians has to say about the heavenly realms, not least because 6:10-20 has yet to be studied, but the leader must be aware of the confusion which may remain hidden in the minds of many who have not understood what Paul explains.

Suggested Questions

1. What is the mystery of Christ and to whom is it revealed?

2. What does Paul say about his experience of the grace of God?

3. What two responsibilities were given to Paul in his ministry?

4. What is God's intention *now* for the church?

5. From what you have understood from the letter so far, what is the manifold wisdom of God? (see 1:8; 1:11-13; 2:19-22)

6. What do we discover elsewhere about the rulers and authorities in the heavenly realms? (see 1:3; 1:20-21; 2:6; 6:12)

7. What is God's eternal purpose? (v. 11)

8. How could Paul's experience of imprisonment (v. 13) be for the Ephesians' glory?

9. What do these verses tell us about church?

10. How might you 'do church' differently as a result?

6

IT IS POSSIBLE (3:14-21)

Thus far the description of church with which we have been presented may seem a long way from our experience. We often don't feel, or act, as this wonderful, harmonious, united body. In fact, often we find church quite difficult. That is why this short section is so important. It is a prayer which expresses the confidence that the impossible can be made possible.

Preliminary observations

There are two significant prayers in this letter. The first (1:15-23) focuses on the power which God has exerted in order to make the church and it is placed before the teaching about what God has done. The second (3:14-21) focuses on the power available to live as the church and comes before the section of the letter which teaches us what that means. Paul's desire is that we, as the church, might be empowered in the very core of our being by the Spirit in order that we would become more like Christ, strengthened by the wonder and magnitude of his love.

Both prayers make it clear that God has done and can do what is impossible with man: create a new people and enable that people to live rightly, to 'be what we are.' And as that for which Paul prays becomes a reality, so the glory of God will be seen in the church and in Christ Jesus. It is for this reason that we must be careful to locate the wonderful doxology at the end of this section firmly in the context of this prayer (3:20-21). Standing alone we may find these verses a great encouragement, but as we see them rooted in that for which Paul prays we begin to realise that the lofty expectations of what it means to be God's people are not unattainable goals. God can do immeasurably more than all we ask or imagine.

Listening to the text

> (14) For this reason I kneel before the Father, (15) from whom his whole family in heaven and earth derives its name. (16) I pray that out of his glorious riches he may strengthen you with power through his Spirit in your inner being, (17) so that Christ may dwell in your hearts through faith. And I pray that you, being rooted and established in love, (18) may have power, together with all the saints, to grasp how wide and long and high and deep is the love of Christ, (19) and to know this love that surpasses knowledge – that you may be filled to the measure of all the fullness of God. (20) Now to him who is able to do immeasurably more than all we ask or imagine, according to his power that is at work within us, (21) to him be glory in the church and in Christ Jesus throughout all generations, for ever and ever! Amen.

Paul begins where he left off in 3:1. Having reminded the Ephesians of what God has done to make the church and of his own calling to make that gospel known, Paul is driven to prayer. It a healthy reminder for those of us who preach that Paul's own calling and commitment to bring the gospel to the Gentiles (3:7-10) was seen not only in his proclamation but also in his prayers. 'For this reason' (the gospel and his responsibility in bringing it to the Ephesians), Paul prays.

In many ways the content of this prayer is an expansion of the prayer of chapter one (1:15-23), in which Paul asks God that the Ephesians may have the Spirit of wisdom to *know* and understand the power that made them the church. Here there is a similar request for power and knowledge, but in such a way that the truth of what he has been explaining might become their *experience* and thus manifest in the practical day to day reality of being a church. It suitably concludes the first part of the letter, linking us back with the great hymn of praise in 1:3-14 and preparing us for the practical teaching of how this might be worked out in church life.

The motivation for prayer (3:14-15)

Although Paul appears to have started his prayer in 3:1, and thus to be linking his reason for praying directly to God's grace in forming the church, the additional autobiographical interlude of 3:2-13 has provided further cause for prayer. Not only has God called the Gentiles to be part of his new community, but he has chosen Paul as the agent to make that known and commissioned him to be his servant to bring that about. Paul's prayer is part of his God-given authority to make the mystery of Christ known to the Gentiles.

To that end this prayer may be directed primarily to the Gentiles. In 3:1 he has their understanding in mind, a concern which Paul might well have carried through to the end of 3:19 before reverting again to the 'big picture' of the church. As the Gentiles experience the life-changing power of God so the body of Christ will be seen in all its fullness and the glory of God will be seen in the church.

The section begins in 3:14 with Paul expressing his posture whilst praying. We may be quite familiar with the idea of kneeling to pray, but the usual Jewish practice would have been to stand. The fact that Paul mentions his body position when praying may well be because he wanted the Gentiles to understand the fervency of his prayer or to remind them of the nature and character of God. The radical news of the revealed mystery of God necessitated exceptional intercession.

It is God the Father before whom he kneels, described in 3:15 as the one 'from whom his whole family in heaven and earth derives its name.' This NIV translation has assumed that Paul was concerned to demonstrate that God has made the church, that his one 'family' in heaven and earth finds its origin in him. True though this certainly is, a more accurate translation presents us with God the Father 'from whom every fatherhood in heaven and on earth is named.' Perhaps Paul wanted to remind the Ephesians that all fatherhood is dependent on the ultimate fatherhood of God; that he is the one with all authority and power and that all family groupings, whether the powers and authorities in the heavenly realms, or the family groupings on earth, are under his rule. In a world where Christians are sidelined and persecuted, it is heartening to know that God is both sovereign and powerful.

A prayer for strength through God's Spirit (3:16-17a)
The first petition in this prayer is for inner strength through God's Spirit. In Paul's earlier prayer (1:15-22), he

prayed that the Ephesians might have the Spirit of wisdom and revelation (1:17) in order that they might know and understand the power which rescued them from sin and alienation in order to make the church. Here he prays that they might experience that power of the Spirit in order that they would be made 'mighty' in the inner man. There is a move from head to heart, from understanding to action.

The riches of his glory (or his glorious riches, NIV) are the limitless resources which make this possible. We have already seen something of what this means in the chapters which have preceded this prayer. In Christ we have every spiritual blessing (1:3), we have been redeemed according to the riches of his grace (1:7), Paul has prayed that we might know and understand the riches of his glorious inheritance in the saints (1:18). It is from this treasure house that Paul asks God for power in order that believers might become mighty.

The way in which believers will be empowered is by the work of the Spirit. He is the agent by which the blessings that are in Christ come to us – we have every spiritual blessing (1:3) and he is the one who guarantees what is yet to come (1:13-14). The church is therefore already Spirit-filled, a living 'temple' (2:22; 5:18) and in that sense we are already in Christ and he is in us. But nevertheless Paul prays that by power and through the work of the Spirit we would be strengthened, made mighty in the inner man.

This uniquely Pauline phrase 'the inner man' relates to the centre of what we are. It is what shapes us and drives us; the centre of our identity and life. Here the work of the Spirit makes us more like Christ and makes the great truths of chapters 1 and 2 more of a reality in the life of the believer. Contrary to the NIV, verses 16 and 17 are not linked by the word 'so.' Paul has reminded us that the believer has already been raised with Christ and that the church, Christ's body, is already the fullness of him who fills everything in every way (1:23). Christ's dwelling in our hearts is not dependent on a subsequent power encounter with the Holy Spirit. Rather, we should read the second part of verse 16 and the first part of verse 17 as parallel clauses which remind us that the experience of the Spirit and the strengthening work of Christ are, in effect, the same activity. Paul is therefore praying for Christians to experience the reality of Christ dwelling in them in order that they may be strengthened and equipped to live this new life, the life of the church; a life which will be unpacked in the remaining chapters of the letter. For this to happen, the Spirit must work.

A prayer for understanding of the love of Christ (3:17b-19)

The second petition builds on the first. Paul has already reminded his readers that 'Because of his great love for us, God, who is rich in mercy, has made us alive in Christ even when we were dead in transgressions and sins' (2:4-5). In that sense those who are in Christ are already established in his love. But this is the love into which 'their life is to be rooted ... the foundation on which their life is to be built.'[1] His choice of foundational words (rooted and grounded in love) reminds them of the truth of what they are, but the Ephesians still need to know and experience what is true of them. Power (or better 'strength') is required in order that the church might understand the extent of the love of Christ. Hence this second petition.

Paul's concern is not only for a personal experience of the love of Christ, but for a corporate understanding which affects the life of the church. Once again he uses the

1   Stott, *Ephesians*, p. 136.

expression, 'all the saints,' which elsewhere refers to the Jew-Gentile brotherhood of the new community (1:1, 15; 6:18). The fact that Paul started his prayer with the Gentiles in mind (3:1) might suggest that he is once again thinking about the wonder of the new Jew-Gentile relationship brought about by the creation of the church. We saw in chapter 1 how the Gentiles were 'also included in Christ' (1:12) and in chapter 2 how those who were alienated and without hope were made into a new people, the church. Chapter 3 again drew our attention to the special ministry of Paul to the Gentiles; and now as he prays for them he once again draws in the rest of the church, those who were Jews and are now 'in Christ.' Hence this prayer is a prayer for the church to be the church. Paul wants all Christians to know Christ's love.

Those who read other commentaries or who look at the original text may be confused as to why Paul omits an object to his four-fold list of dimensions. Literally, his prayer is for 'what is the breadth and length and height and depth and to know the love of Christ excelling knowledge.' Whilst a number of suggestions have been made, it seems perfectly reasonable to assume Paul is speaking about the magnitude of the love of Christ: the whole letter rests on an understanding of all that we have in Christ (1:3); the church is his body, the fullness of him who fills everything in every way (1:23); Paul's desire is that Christians might be filled to the measure of all the fullness of God (3:19b) and is at pains to explain how that might happen in the following verses, the end point of which is maturity, described as 'the whole measure of the fullness of Christ.' (4:13). Given that this concern runs throughout the letter, the fourfold desire of 'breadth, length, height and depth' almost certainly relates to the love of Christ.

But herein lies a paradox. Paul prays that Christians might know a love which is greater than knowledge; a love which is inexhaustible. Rather than being a contradiction, it is a great reminder that the love of Christ is of such a magnitude that we will never fully understand or grasp it. But only as we are strengthened and empowered by God to live as the Church will we begin to understand it. We are 'filled to the measure of all the fullness of God' as, with the church, we are strengthened by the Spirit to live out what is true of us and as our heavenly Father grants us more insight and understanding. That is the goal of the prayer. His desire is Christian maturity. Here, on the interface between theology and practice, Paul prays that the theological truths of chapters 1 and 2 about the love of God in creating the church (1:4; 2:4) and the nature of the church as the 'fullness' of Christ (1:22-23), might be experienced in the life of the church.

God can do it (3:20-21)

As we understand this prayer and begin to think through its implications, we could perhaps be forgiven for wondering whether this is really possible. As we look at our fellowships with the mess and muddle of church life, the difficult people, the failure to evangelise or to integrate new Christians, the back-biting, gossip and factions, we might begin to ask if this wonderful picture of church can ever become a reality. That is why we need to take 3:20-21 to heart. Far from being a rather memorable liturgical conclusion to a prayer meeting, these words confirm to us that what Paul has just prayed for can become a reality.

Paul has made it clear that God has already done immeasurably more than all we ask or imagine. When dead, we were made alive; when alienated, we were reconciled.

A new entity, the church, has come into being. At the same time, we are a work in progress. The reality of what we are is still being worked out in our midst. Paul has not yet told us exactly how this will happen or what we need to do if it is to become a reality (that will come in the following chapters), but nevertheless, God is able to do immeasurably more than all we ask or imagine. The power for which Paul prays – to be Christlike (by the work of his Spirit in the inner man) and to grasp the love of Christ inexhaustible though it is – is available and is at work. Practically it will be seen as we begin to understand the magnitude of the love of God and who we are in Christ. That is the start-point for Christian maturity. And when that happens, the riches of his glory which have brought it about (3:16) will be seen in the church (1:21) and therefore in Christ Jesus, whose body, the church, is the fullness of him who fills everything in every way (1:23).

This extraordinary grace-driven action of God will last through eternity, throughout all generations. As this prayer is answered, so what God has done will be seen in our midst. Satan will shudder, the rulers and authorities in the heavenlies will see the wisdom of God, and we will become what God wants us to be, a picture of his purposes for all eternity.

And so we stand on the threshold of Paul's application with a prayer, linking the theological truth of chapters 1 and 2 (what we are) to the practical reality of chapters 4-6 (how we become what we are).

From text to teaching

Many people will know this prayer but will probably not see how it fits within the context of Ephesians. It is important to communicate that this is the interface between the theological reality of what we are (chapters 1 and 2), which Paul wants them to know and understand, and the outworking of that truth in the life of the church (chapters 4-6), which he wants them to experience. The apparently impossible task of being the church becomes possible through an understanding of the power of God experienced through the limitless love of Christ. Central to our understanding of the whole letter is what God has done in Christ, that in him we have every spiritual blessing and that his church is his body, the fullness of him who fills everything in every way.

Without understanding what we already have, this prayer seems to ask for unattainable things. Only when we understand that it arises from what we already have will the desired outworking of what it means to be church become possible, both in terms of the new *walk* of 2:10 and in what Paul is about to teach. God really will do more than all we ask or imagine; and thereby his glory will be manifest in the church and in Christ Jesus for ever and ever.

Introduction

If we are to be as consistent as possible with the letter to the Ephesians we will have to work hard to ensure that this wonderful prayer is located firmly in its context. It arises from Paul's concern for Gentile understanding of the gospel and its implications and is an extension of his ministry to them. Having spent two chapters clarifying what it means to be God's new humanity this prayer is asking God to make the experience of what we are become a reality in the church. Depending on the situation into which we are preaching we might begin a sermon by creating a mental picture of the perfect church and asking whether it could ever come about, or, perhaps more challengingly, ask people to think what it is that shapes the content of our own prayers, most of which are unlikely to be a concern for the glory of God within the local church.

Preaching outline – examples

The prayer falls naturally into four sections, as suggested in the examples below. As suggested elsewhere, the style and nature of titles are often personal to the preacher and need not be prescriptively stated. Whether we use the conclusion to each point as the title (in order to help people to remember the application) or create alliterative sequences is very much a personal matter. The key thing is to engage rightly with the text and speak into the culture of our hearers.

Possible outlines:

1. God's work – a drive to prayer (3:14-15)

2. Power from the Spirit (3:16-17a)

3. Power to grasp the love of Christ (3:17b-19)

4. God will do it (3:20-21)

Or, with slightly different headings:

1. Prayer to a sovereign God (3:14-15)

2. Prayer for spiritual strength (3:16-17a)

3. Prayer for grasping limitless love (3:17b-19)

4. The God who will do more (3:20-21)

Application

One obvious implication of these truths is that we must pray as Paul prayed. The content of Biblical prayers should inform and direct the content and manner of our prayers.

Equally, we see something of the possibility for the church as that prayer is answered. The real, practical outworking of what it means to be church, where the glory of God will be seen and the wisdom of God manifest, is not an unattainable goal. Human effort will not bring it about, but a church resourced in the riches of Christ can begin to manifest some of these realities.

What is particularly striking in these words is the fact that without the power of God we will not grasp the love of Christ. The limitless nature of such love cannot be comprehended, not only because of its magnitude, but also because it is spiritually discerned. But as we begin to grasp the love of God shown in Jesus Christ, then we will grow into his fullness; we will become mature.

The implications for the church are profound. This is a prayer for the church, not simply for individuals, a prayer to which we must return time and time again as we are being built together to become a dwelling in which God lives by his Spirit.

Questions for home groups/study groups

Leading studies on this passage will present similar challenges to preaching it. Many will know this prayer, or part of this prayer, but may not have connected it to the rest of the letter. It is, therefore, important to allow the letter to inform us about the riches of God (in Christ), the love of God and the fullness of God (in Christ). We will need to show how the placing of the prayer on the interface of theology and practice sets us up for what is about to come; and we will also need to realise that when we come to understand what this prayer is about, we will realise that the love of Christ surpasses knowledge. It must be understood and experienced but only when we realise its magnitude will we begin to grow into the people God wants us to be. The time of prayer with which many groups conclude an evening's study will need to be handled wisely and scripturally. The ultimate consequence of what we read here will be that God is glorified in our midst.

Suggested questions

1. Think carefully about the content of your prayers. What do you normally pray about? How do you decide what to pray for?

2. What is the motivation for Paul's prayer?

3. For whom is Paul praying?

4. How might you explain 3:19 in the light of 1:23?

5. What is Paul's main concern in this prayer? How will we see it being answered in our church if we pray this prayer?

6. How does 3:20 encourage us in the light of what Paul has been praying in 3:14-19?

7. Read again the first prayer (1:15-23) alongside this prayer. Why does Paul pray as he does? Why is this prayer here?

8. What does this prayer teach us about our prayers?

9. How might your prayer-life change in the light of this prayer?

7
HOW TO BE MATURE (4:1-16)

These few verses are fundamental to Paul's letter because they tell us how our identity in Christ (Chapters 1 and 2) can become reality in our experience. We know that such change is possible because Paul has just stated that the God to whom he prays will do immeasurably more than all we ask or imagine. Our status in Christ is not simply a theological idea; it is a life-changing reality which can and should be seen in the local fellowships of which we are a part.

Preliminary observations

As we move to the so-called ethical section of the letter, we must be careful not to drive too large a wedge between theology and practice. The first half of the book has been full of what it means to be the church and we have already had various hints as to what that might look like. Now the reality is spelled out more clearly. Having grasped what God has done in Christ we are now about to be told how we live out what we already are. Paul is embarking on a significant section in which he explains what the Lord has given the church in order that we might live as his reconciled and redeemed people.

A sermon on this section could continue to 4:24. Thereafter the teaching becomes much more practical and sets forth what this new life looks like, in our relationships in church, with the world and in the domestic sphere (wives and husbands, children and parents, slaves and masters). However, there is so much in this section, and it is of such importance for our understanding of what it means to be church, that it is probably best to end at 4:16.

Listening to the text

(1) As a prisoner for the Lord, then, I urge you to live a life worthy of the calling you have received. (2) Be completely humble and gentle; be patient, bearing with one another in love. (3) Make every effort to keep the unity of the Spirit through the bond of peace. (4) There is one body and one Spirit – just as you were called to one hope when you were called – (5) one Lord, one faith, one baptism; (6) one God and father of all, who is over all and through all and in all. (7) But to each one of us grace has been given as Christ apportioned it. (8) This is why it says: 'When he ascended on high he led captives in his train and gave gifts to men.' (9) (What does 'he ascended' mean except that he also descended to the lower, earthly regions? (10) He who descended is the very one who ascended higher than all the heavens in order to fill the whole universe.) (11) It was he who gave some to be apostles, some to be prophets, some to be evangelists, and some to be pastors and teachers, (12) to prepare God's people for works of

service, so that the body of Christ may be built up (13) until we all reach unity in the faith and in the knowledge of the Son of God and become mature, attaining to the whole measure of the fullness of Christ. (14) Then we will no longer be infants, tossed back and forth by the waves, and blown here and there by every wind of teaching and by the cunning and craftiness of men in their deceitful scheming. (15) Instead, speaking the truth in love, we will in all things grow up into him who is the Head, that is, Christ. (16) From him the whole body, joined and held together by every supporting ligament, grows and builds itself up in love, as each part does its work.

The normal Christian life (4:1-6)

God has called us to be part of this radical new community – that is the calling Christians have received. The NIV wording might lead us to think that our Christian living is no more than response to God's grace ('I urge you to live a life worthy of the calling you have received'), providing us with a form of debtor's ethic which drives us to better living. But contrary to the familiar idea of 'the debt of love which is owed by this thankful heart,' Ephesians reminds us that even our response to the calling of God is empowered by grace. The grace of God has already achieved everything for our Christian living. We have to do no more than *walk* in those works which God has already prepared for us (the Word which is used in 2:10). It is the power and grace of God, in knowledge and experience, that can make these ethical standards the norm in our churches.

A right understanding of what drives and empowers our Christian living will save us, on the one hand from the idea that God, having done all, awaits to see how we will respond, and on the other hand from the idea that we can just 'let

go and let God.' Instead, we will see that the grace which
rescues us is the grace which equips us and the grace that
will 'lead us home.' Even our desire to submit to God's Word
and the effort we put in to obeying it are themselves signs
of God's grace. We must make the effort to live rightly, but
we can only do so because of the empowering grace of God,
for which Paul has prayed in the preceding verses. That is
why we are not called to create unity, but rather to maintain
the unity which has already been created for us in Christ.
This is something which 'human beings cannot create; it is
given to them, but their responsibility is to keep it, to guard
it in the face of many attempts from within and without the
church to take it away.'[1] We need to be reminded that 'the
unity of the church is as indestructible as the unity of God
himself. It is no more possible to split the church than it is
possible to split the Godhead.'[2] We are simply called to 'live
a life worthy of the calling we have received.'

That said, the standards are very high. Five qualities
are mentioned: lowliness (or humility), meekness (or
gentleness), patience, forbearance and love, all of which
mark us out as a people made new in Christ, created to
walk in love (1:4). This last attribute 'is the basic attitude of
seeking the highest good of others and it will therefore lead
to all these qualities and include them all.'[3]

Complete humility, patience and a love which bears all
may be 'the foundational stones of Christian unity'[4] but
they are qualities rarely seen in many of our churches. Sadly,
Christians often experience quite the opposite. The oneness

---

1   F Foulkes, *Tyndale New Testament Commentary: Ephesians*
(Nottingham, UK: IVP, 1989) p. 117.
2   Stott, *Ephesians*, p. 151.
3   Foulkes, *Ephesians*, p. 116-17.
4   Stott, *Ephesians*, p. 149.

which Paul stresses – one body, one Spirit, one hope, one Lord, one faith, one baptism, one God and Father of all – is either lost in endlessly elaborated doctrinal divisions, or it is assumed to mean that unity must be seen at any cost, regardless of what truth may be abandoned in the process. Somehow, neither extreme sits happily with the presentation of the church which has been given to us thus far in this letter. Something different is going on; something which relates to the Lord Jesus and what he has given to his church to make this reality a possibility.

If we were to take these few verses without understanding how they fit into this section as a whole we would find them very difficult to preach. It would become almost impossible to determine the parameters which should be applied to the unity of the church. The Bible does not hold to unity at all costs. When Jesus prayed for future believers (John 17:20-21) he had in mind those who would believe the message preached by the apostles, the same message which is foundational to the church in Ephesians. Yet not all who professed faith were authentic members of his church. It is possible to call Jesus 'Lord' and yet not end up being saved (Matt. 7:21-23). The qualifying factor is obedience to the preached Word (Matt. 7:24-27), just as we will see in this chapter of Paul's letter. His teaching must shape our understanding of what constitutes 'unity', without which we may inadvertently project onto these words a concept of unity which does not come from the Bible and cannot be sustained by it.

Paul's approach is somewhat different. Whilst he presents a very high view of what the church should be in these verses, connecting unity with the qualities of lowliness, meekness, patience, forbearance and love, he goes

on to spell out how they might be achieved. We get a hint of
this if we glance down to 4:13-16. At the beginning of the
section we are urged to keep the unity won for us (4:3); by
the end of the section such unity (4:13) and love (4:15-16)
are assumed and achieved. The intervening verses tell us
how that happens.

Gifts from the risen Lord (4:7-10)

This short section begins by reminding us that the risen
Jesus equips his church to be his church. All we need is in
him; and his grace is given to all those who belong to him so
that each person within his church is empowered to behave
and act in a way which will build the church.

The verse quoted by Paul comes from Psalm 68:18
which, in its Old Testament context, is a call for God to
arise and scatter his enemies, reminding readers both of
his gracious rescue in the past and of his victorious power.
The result of this is that God leads his captives in triumph,
probably to the temple mount.

In order to understand what might have been in Paul's
mind as he wrote these words we need to look at his own
explanation, as given in verses 9-10. Many in the early
church assumed that Paul was thinking of Jesus' descent
into Hades, especially in the light of Paul's choice of words
which speak of Jesus descending to the 'lower parts of the
earth.' Though there is a debate about this doctrine, there
is nothing in Ephesians to suggest this was in Paul's mind.

More recently some have assumed that Paul was speaking
about the giving of the Spirit. Psalm 68 was often associated
with Moses' ascent of Mount Sinai in order to receive the
law and was, therefore, often used liturgically at the feast of
Pentecost, which celebrated the giving of the law. As a result
some Jewish teaching went further, assuming that Moses

ascended into heaven to receive the law before descending to earth in order to give it to the people. In the same way Jesus gave the Spirit once he had ascended, thereby enabling those who belong to him to live a life worthy of the calling they have received. Attractive though this might be, verses 9 and 10 make it clear that Paul is speaking here about the descent of Christ rather than the Spirit. He is the one who descended to the earthy regions before ascending on high.

The most likely explanation is that, just as Psalm 68 reminds us that Yahweh descended to deliver his people and triumph over his enemies before ascending to heaven, so Christ descended to the earth in order to secure a victory over sin and death before ascending into heaven. The 'lower earthly regions' remind us of the humility of Jesus, making himself nothing and becoming obedient to death on a cross. In his death he secured a victory and now he holds the highest possible honour and glory. Indeed, without his death he would not be able to do what he now does, that is to equip his church in order to be the people he wants us to be. His descent is not simply a precursor to his ascent, but the means of securing the people to whom he now gives gifts.

This understanding not only fits with the rest of the letter (1:21-22) but also helps us to understand how Paul can appear to 'modify' the words of Psalm 68. In its original context God receives gifts rather than giving them, but he does so because those who are defeated recognise who he is; even his enemies acknowledge his victory. Likewise the victory of Jesus is total; he has ascended higher than all the heavens in order to fill the whole universe. Perhaps, too, there is a hint of ancient military practice in which the victor would distribute the plunder to the armies who

fought for them. Jesus has been raised; he has power over all
authorities, he fills the whole universe, he has won a people
by his descent to earth and his death on the cross. He now
has all power and authority to equip them as his people.

In this sense these few verses are critical for Paul's
argument. Jesus has won a people for himself and he has
the power and ability to equip them as his people. How this
happens in the local church and the gifts he gives to bring
this about are the subject of the next section.

Attaining maturity (4:11-16)

Once it has been established that the one who came to earth
and has now ascended as Lord of all has given gifts to his
church, these gifts are spelled out. Whilst the various lists
of gifts elsewhere in the New Testament are more extensive,
the gifts mentioned here relate entirely to Word ministry:
apostles, prophets, evangelists, pastors and teachers.

Apostles and prophets (4:11a)

We have discovered already that the church is built on the
foundation of the apostles and prophets (2:20) and that
they are the ones to whom the message of the gospel has
been given (3:5). It was their proclaimed message which
brought the church into being and their message which
is now contained in this letter. The apostles and prophets
are not some ongoing group of specially endowed people
in the present-day church, but rather those people who
are uniquely qualified to bring the message of the gospel
(which was given to them) to the world, as Paul made clear
in 3:2-13.

There has been a degree of debate as to the identity of
the prophets. They cannot be Old Testament prophets as
we know them, because Paul speaks of them as receiving

insights not known until his own generation (3:5).Yet they
cannot be a group that continued indefinitely, either, as the
foundation of 2:20 has been laid once and is not being laid
continuously.

We should be cautious about building a theology of
prophecy from a single word in the letter. In other letters
Paul does discuss prophecy at greater length, and it is
possible that the prophets to whom he is referring here can
be identified with them, but Paul's point in this letter is that
the Lord Jesus has given the unique revelation of the gospel
to these people - the message which creates and sustains
the church. His purpose is to remind the church that they
already have everything they need to be the church and to
live as a unified, loving and mature people.

Evangelists (4:11b)

Whilst apostles and prophets were foundational in that
they were recipients of the revealed mystery of the gospel,
the ministry of evangelists, pastors and teachers was and
is ongoing. An evangelist must be a proclaimer of the
apostolic message, whether or not they themselves heard
it directly from an apostle. This might be an itinerant
ministry, travelling around or being sent out by the local
congregation to break new ground, but it might also be
a 'local' ministry, as with Timothy who was asked to stay in
Ephesus (1 Tim. 1:3), but who was asked to do the work of
an evangelist (2 Tim. 4:5).

These words suggest that some people will be specifically
gifted as evangelists, but it must be remembered that all God's
people are called to evangelise. Not only must we be ready
to give an answer for the hope that we have (1 Pet. 3:15)
but we must also be intentional in our desire to share the
gospel. In the Acts of the Apostles all Christians spoke the

Word of God (Acts 8:4); Paul's letter to the Philippians speaks of the encouragement the brothers had for their own evangelism in seeing Paul evangelise (Phil. 1:14). The gifting of some does not mean that others should not or cannot share their faith. The Lord's message should 'ring out' from all authentic churches (1 Thess. 1:8).

We need constant reminders of the gospel and constant encouragement to proclaim it. In including evangelists here, Paul is demonstrating how the risen Lord Jesus makes, sustains and builds the church: just as the truth required to make the church has been revealed to the apostles and prophets, so now that truth must be proclaimed for the church to grow.

Pastors and teachers (4:11c)
Once the non-Christian has heard the evangel (the gospel message which has been given to the apostles and prophets and proclaimed by the evangelists) and responded to it, he or she will then be a part of the church, which then needs to be nurtured and taught by pastors and teachers.

As these two gifts are bracketed together it seems reasonable to assume that they are not two separate offices – all authentic pastors will teach; all authentic teachers will pastor. Whilst the metaphor of shepherding is widely applied in both the Old Testament and the New, the predominant activities of the pastor-teacher will be to feed sheep (by teaching correctly), to seek lost sheep (by searching for sinners to repent) and to protect sheep from false teaching. His role model will be that of the Lord Jesus who, in fulfilling the expectations of the authentic shepherding from the Old Testament (eg Ezek. 34:11-16), demonstrated what it means to shepherd the flock (John 10:1-18; 1 Pet. 2:25). As Jesus taught (Mark 1:38) and commissioned his apostles to do the same (Matt. 28:18-20; John 21:15-17), so the pastor-teacher models himself on Jesus (1 Pet. 5:2-4) and teaches the flock (2 Tim. 4:1-4). Likewise, just as the mission of Jesus and his apostles concerned the lost (Luke 15, Acts 2 etc.) so also the ministry of the pastor-teacher will involve seeking the lost (2 Tim. 4:5). Finally, just as the ministry of Jesus constantly corrected the misunderstandings of the religious teaching of his day (eg. Mark 7) so too the role of the pastor-teacher requires constant vigilance against the perils of false teaching (Acts 20:29; 2 Tim. 4:3; Titus 1:9).

All who have become part of the church as a result of hearing the revealed message (i.e. the result of the ministry of evangelists) need pastors and teachers in order to be equipped to be God's church. 'Initial [gifts] are the "apostles and prophets" who founded the congregations by their preaching and spiritual words, secured them in the Word of Christ and thus themselves represented the foundation of the church (2:20). But then the preachers, pastors and teachers... carry on the preaching, careful guidance and teaching. They are intended... for the preparation of the saints i.e. the faithful, and consequently perform a continuing service which is meant to benefit the development of Christ's body.'[5]

The purpose of Word ministry (4:12-13)
The purpose of these Word gifts is given in 4:12. It is to prepare God's people for works of service (literally: works of ministry). The risen Lord Jesus enables his church to grow (in number and maturity) by equipping people to proclaim and teach his Word. The purpose of these Word ministries is to equip Christians for ministry, for Christian service. And as Christians serve in the local church by ministering

---

5   Rudolph Schnackenburg, *The Epistle to the Ephesians* (Edinburgh, UK: T&T Clark, 1991) p.190.

to one another, so the unity which has been brought about through the blood of Christ, the unity of the Spirit which we are asked to maintain, becomes possible.

It is important to be clear about what Paul says here. The Word proclaimed through the gifts mentioned does not grow the church directly. Rather, the Word equips the church members (to whom God's grace has been apportioned) to minister in service to one another. Only then does the church grow into unity and maturity, attaining to the whole measure of the fullness of Christ.

When Christians serve, that which we have in Christ (1:3-14), that which we are in Christ (1:23) becomes that which people see. The earthly church increasingly presents a picture of the heavenly reality when those who profess faith in Christ live in obedience to his Word by serving one another. 'In his beneficial filling of the church (1:23) he takes individual people into his service, each for a particular task, arranges them in the whole, with the goal of unity and thus himself provides for the development of the body.'[6]

However, the nature of this ministry, this service, is not explained at this point in the letter. Here we are given the principles of how the Lord Jesus organises his church to be what he has made us to be. The remainder of the letter will explain how we should relate to one another (for example 5:21), and whilst this chapter does highlight something of the nature of Christian relationships (4:2, 25-27, 28, 29, 31, 32), we also need to use Biblical common sense from the rest of the New Testament if we are to understand what 'ministry' to one another looks like. As we do so we will see that 'ministry' refers both to 'charitable service' and to serving the Lord himself. Both these are needed if the

---

6   Schnackenburg, *Ephesians*, p. 190.

church is to grow to maturity; both flow from obedience to the Word he has given as taught by those gifted by him.

The effect of Word ministry (4:14-16)

As Christians begin to serve in this way, so the church becomes the loving body we are called to be, the world sees we are disciples, and the principalities and powers recognise the wisdom of God being worked out in our midst. The Biblical expectation of normal Christianity is service in response to the Word so that individuals grow into the likeness of Christ and the church grows into the people God has made us to be.

Ephesians 4:13 explains how the effect of the Word obeyed will produce unity and maturity. The contrast to this is given in 4:14. If we do not obey the Word in acts of ministry, which lead to unity and maturity, then we will be like children, infantile in our faith and open to every wind of teaching. The contrast is between the mature person and the child and the metaphor adopted visually expresses the peril of adopting the latter's mindset. We will end up 'unstable, lacking direction, vacillating, and open to manipulation... like small, rudderless boats'[7]. The only way to prevent such danger is by total obedience to the given Word.

Some have ascribed the winds of teaching which blew around Ephesus to 'various religious philosophies which threatened to undermine or dilute the apostolic gospel'[8]. The threats which face us may be different, but common to all is the undermining work of Satan: the same word for 'craftiness' in 4:14 is used directly of the devil in 6:11. Satan has always sought to distort the Word – and when he does so, wrong behaviour follows, as we shall see later in the letter.

---

7   O'Brien, *Ephesians*, p. 308.
8   O'Brien, *Ephesians*, p. 309.

Presumably the lack of any specific situation makes this a general instruction, a warning against the subtle distortion of truth. Paul realised that such erroneous teaching was persuasive enough to be able to tempt Christians away from the truth; they and we need to be reminded of the gospel and to be rigorous in our faithfulness to the truth, which will always be seen in acts of ministry to one another.

As we engage in right ways with the Word, the realities of 4:15 should be seen in our midst. Unlike false teachers who speak error and have cunning and crafty ways, the authentic Christian is right in content (speaking the truth) and in manner (doing so in love). The original has the feel of 'truthing in love' which, obviously, cannot happen without the truth being articulated. The church must adhere to the gospel which has been given to the apostles and prophets. Only when that happens will we grow into the one who is head both of the church and the universe. Once again, the language is of maturity. That is God's desire for his people – Christian maturity.

Ephesians 4:16 makes this abundantly clear. Returning to the ideas of 4:7, knowing that all people are empowered by grace to serve, we are presented with a wonderful picture of the church. Everyone is joined together and everyone serves. Paul describes the body as held together and supported by ligaments so that 'it is clear that the union and growth of the body can only come when there is contact with other members of the body. Although the body is one, the members are distinct. However, interaction between members, as gifts are exercised, promotes both individual and corporate growth. Every believer is necessary to this process, not just a select few.'[9]

---

9   Harold W. Hoehner, *Ephesians An Exegetical Commentary* (Grand Rapids, USA: Baker Academic, 2002) p. 573.

Each person within the church community, the body of Christ, is to function with 'the grace that has been given as Christ apportioned it.' Only then will we become the loving community we were designed to be. Verses 4:12-13 will then become a reality – we will be loving and we will be unified. But without such service, the body of Christ cannot grow properly.

From text to teaching

Introduction

Many of us belong to congregations which are used to Bible teaching. We easily assess the soundness of churches by what is said from the pulpit, and rightly so, but these verses will not allow us to stop there. The mark of an authentic, growing church is whether or not those who hear the Word demonstrate their obedience to it by ministering to one another. Without that grace-empowered Word response we may end up being members of very immature churches even if the preaching is sound. The challenge in this passage is, therefore, enormous; and whilst we do not want to chide those to whom we preach we cannot help but consider how our introduction might challenge our sense of spiritual satisfaction. We may think we are mature, but are we ministering to one another? We may think we are a Biblical church, but are we becoming more unified and loving? Equally, we may realise all too painfully that we are not growing, that we are not unified or loving and we may need the gentle instruction of these verses to remedy our spiritual malaise.

Without knowing our congregation it will be all too easy to take the wrong approach or to disconnect the earlier part of the letter from the later chapters. Paul begins by begging, urging the congregation to walk according to their calling to be God's people, made possible only because of the work of the risen Lord Jesus, manifest in the Word ministries within his church.

Explanation

What has been achieved in the heavenly realm, in Christ, becomes visible in the earthly realm, his body, the church, as Christians obey the Word by ministering to one another. The fullness which is already ours in Christ (1:23) becomes visible as we obey the Word by serving.

Many of us have very individualistic views of salvation and therefore a rather incomplete view of the church. In his commentary Muddiman makes the comment that: 'Perhaps even more insidious is the modern Western tendency to treat faith as a private matter and to judge the church by its utility (or otherwise) in lending support to the religious preferences of the individual. Against this Ephesians protests that salvation is essentially corporate; we are saved together or not at all.'[10]

That has profound implications for what it means to be church. In evangelical circles we often speak about Bible *teaching* churches; but what we really want is Bible obeying churches, because only by *obeying* what the Word says is the church equipped for ministry and only as the church ministers can we become what we are. It is not the Word that builds the church directly. Rather, the Word builds those who are part of the church so that they serve; and as they serve one another, so the church becomes what it is in Christ. Without such a pattern of ministry, we will just be infants, mere children. We will never grow up in our faith.

---

10   John Muddiman, *The Epistle to the Ephesians* (London, UK: Continuum, 2001) p. 49.

Our problem is that we tend to view church as a bus rather than an orchestra. There is a driver who does all the work and a series of passengers who enjoy the ride. They often are very proud of their bus; they like good driving and can spot bad driving a mile off. They enjoy their reputation of being a well driven bus perhaps even with a well known driver; he may even have spoken on conferences about how to drive well. They think being on the bus is about having a great time – a buzz every time they meet together.

Many on the bus have been travelling for years but they don't always know those who have got on to the bus at a later stop. In previous years some have helped clean the bus and service the engine, but now they just talk about what they used to do with pride. They still think that it is a good idea to stop and pick new up new passengers, but they feel that it isn't their gift. One or two of them refuse to talk to anyone else on the bus; some are very particular about where they sit and a few just come for the company.

That is often the experience we have of church, but it is not the Biblical picture of what church should be.

Church should be more like an orchestra in which everybody has a part to play if the music is to sound as the composer intended. It is essential for everyone to play from the same score and do what it says, and for a conductor to guide the orchestra through the piece in order to bring out what the composer has written. Only then will the music come alive, only then will the sound made match the intention of its creator. Without a conductor the music may sound haphazard and imprecise; without each instrument playing it is incomplete.

So with the church. We must all play from the same score (the Bible); we must all respond together, serving one another faithfully with the gifts we have received – and we all need a conductor who will rightly teach the Word, interpreting what is set before him in order that we may make the sound the composer intended. There is no place in church for the Christian who listens but does not obey, or the individual who professes faith but does not minister to his fellow believers. And just as it is impossible to be an authentic member of an orchestra without playing an instrument, so it is impossible to be an authentic Christian without serving one another in the local church. But as we obey the Word by works of ministry we become unified, mature and loving, and the principalities and powers in the heavenly realms look down and see 'the wisdom of God' manifest among us (3:10). We need to be Bible-obeying churches if we are to show now what God has made us in Christ, if we are to be a picture of the future – a united, mature people bringing glory to God and causing Satan to quake in his boots.

If this Bible-obeying is not at the heart of our churches we will never be mature; we will never live as the Lord intends his church to be. But when we are obedient, the Word will produce the unity which is already ours in Christ.

Application
Two obvious applications emerge from this passage. The first relates to the teaching and preaching of God's Word. The risen Lord has equipped people within his church to teach the given Word and pastor the congregation. The intentional result of this ministry will be that we become more loving, more unified and less easily blown around by the latest wind of teaching – in other words, that we will become more Christlike. It means that all who preach or teach should a) be rigorous in adhering to given truth,

teaching, correcting and rebuking in order that authentic doctrine is set forth plainly and b) should be gifted and able to do so.

The second application relates to the response to authentic Bible ministry. The expected response to correct teaching is obedient service, which will result primarily in acts of ministry towards one another. The nature of these acts of ministry will vary from person to person, but all are both expected and equipped to serve in this way. A church in which there is wonderful teaching but little or no response is not a Biblical church and will not grow into maturity.

Preaching outline – an example
There are many possible ways of tackling this passage, but it is important to see 4:1-6 as the expected outworking of what it means to be God's people and 4:7-16 as the means by which this happens. We must be cautious of preaching in such a way that grace-given salvation is separate from grace-given living. God makes us what we are and enables us to live as we are.

The shape of the passage determines how we might best divide it. The unity and love expected in the first few verses are made possible at the end of the passage by what happens in between. The risen Christ gives Word-gifts; as the church responds in obedience Christians will be equipped for works of ministry, which in turn enables the church to grow. The precise headings we use will be a matter of personal style and preference but this basic flow of Paul's argument needs to be maintained.

Parts of this passage may require more time, especially if there is some confusion between God's sovereign grace and our response, or legitimate questions about the nature of gifts or indeed how the preaching of God's Word relates to the ministry-response of God's people. It may therefore be wise to spend longer on this section so as to deal with these very real concerns.

1. 4:1-6   What the church should look like

2. 4:7-11   What Jesus has given to enable us to be church

3. 4:12-16   How to become what we are:

                 Listen to the Word

                 Do what it says

Or,

1. 4:1-6   Called to unity and love

2. 4:7-11   Christ: Word gifts given

3. 4:12   Church: Word gifts obeyed

4. 4:13-16   Unity and love achieved

5. Conclusion: What the church should look like

Questions for home groups/study groups

In leading studies on this section I have found it helpful to use a whiteboard so as to show the symmetry of the passage. It begins with the instruction about how to live, most notably to make every effort to keep the unity of the Spirit and to bear with one another in love. It then ends with a picture of a loving and unified church. The intervening verses then become the well from which we drink, telling us how we can do verses 1-6 to become verses 13-16.

1. What does it mean to live a life worthy of the calling you have received?

2. Does this describe our church? If not, why not?

3. In the light of what we have seen so far, why do you think Paul stresses the oneness of verses 4 and 5?

4. What do 4:7-10 tell us about Jesus and the church?

5. What information have we already been given about the ministries in 4:11 (2:20; 3:5)? Can you explain what they are? What does that mean for us?

6. What must God's people do to be mature (compare 4:13 with 4:3)?

7. How do you make sense of 4:13 in the light of 1:23? How do we grow into the fullness which we already have?

8. What is the alternative to maturity (4:14)?

9. How can you be sure you are not an 'infant'?

10. What must we do to become mature and loving (4:15-16)?

11. How does this practically change what we do in church and the part we play in it?

8

DON'T BE A SINNER. BE A SAINT
(4:17-24)

These few verses are Paul's conclusion to what we studied in our last chapter. They serve not only to remind us of the need to keep the Word taught and obeyed at the heart of our lives and churches, but also to warn us of the great peril of not doing so. We have placed before us a stark alternative. Will you live as a sinner or as a saint?

Preliminary observations
Paul's great concern in the second half of the letter is to show how the reality of what God has done in Christ can be seen in the way we live as church. The following sections will take us on a tour of church life, both when we are gathered and as we live in the world and the home. But before Paul begins to tell us what 4:1-3 will look like in those different sets of relationships, he concludes 4:1-16 with a contrast between the Christian whose mind has been changed and informed by the Word obeyed, and the non-Christian whose mind is empty and darkened. As with

all New Testament teaching, we discover that belief always leads to behaviour; and behaviour always indicates whether we have truly believed.

The passage can be split into two sections. The first is a warning not to live as the Gentiles live; the second is a reminder of what is expected in those who have come to Christ and have been made alive in him.

Listening to the text

(17) So I tell you this, and insist on it in the Lord, that you must no longer live as the Gentiles do, in the futility of their thinking. (18) They are darkened in their understanding and separated from the life of God because of the ignorance that is in them due to the hardening of their hearts. (19) Having lost all sensitivity, they have given themselves over to sensuality so as to indulge in every kind of impurity, with a continual lust for more. (20) You, however, did not come to know Christ that way. (21) Surely you heard of him and were taught in him in accordance with the truth that is in Jesus. (22) You were taught, with regard to your former way of life, to put off your old self, which is being corrupted by its deceitful desires; (23) to be made new in the attitude of your minds; (24) and to put on the new self, created to be like God in true righteousness and holiness.

Do not live as the Gentiles do (4:17-19)

It must be noted at the outset how much of this passage relates to the mind. Paul has just explained the centrality of the Word obeyed in the lives of Christians. As they understand and obey, so they grow into the people they were made to be – loving, unified and mature. In contrast, the exhortation here is not to live as the Gentiles do, whose thinking is futile, whose minds are darkened and who are ignorant. It means that those who are not taught, or who do not obey what they hear, put themselves in the category of the unconverted, with catastrophic results. In that sense, we can see how this short section links with what has gone before. Understand and obey the Word and you will grow into Christ-like character; ignore the Word and you will grow into immorality and debauchery.

Once again, therefore, this is about our Christian walk. The NIV chooses not to use the word in verse 17 but in the original the wording is clear: 'no longer walk as the Gentiles walk.' Elsewhere Paul has referred to the non-Jewish Christians as Gentiles (2:11; 3:1) and he has also made it abundantly clear that the gospel is for the Gentiles (3:6, 8), but here the word is used to refer to those who are still dead in sin and subject to the wrath of God. This is what life is like without Christ and it is characterised, first, by futile thinking.

The word used for 'thinking' or 'mind' (ESV) relates not to intellectual ability but rather to a mind-set which is unable to reason, think and decide in ways which result in right living. We might learn much from the non-Christian scientist; we may delight in the creativity and literary genius of the atheistic novelist, but such a mind cannot live God's way. And 'because it lacks true relationships with God, Gentile thinking suffers from the consequences of having lost touch with reality and is left fumbling with inane trivialities and worthless side issues.'[1]

Futile thinking is further explained in verse 18. Non-Christians have darkened understanding so that they are blind to the truth of the gospel. They have been alienated

---

1   O'Brien, *Ephesians*, p.320.

from God (NIV 'separated') by virtue of their ignorance; their hearts have been hardened. The wording of the original suggests that their alienation has two causes, as both phrases, 'because of' and 'due to' are translations of the same word. The first cause of their alienation is their ignorance and the second, which is probably subordinate to the first, is the hardness of their hearts. This is wilful and culpable stubbornness of heart which is not simply external; it is 'in them.' Here is a people who have deliberately suppressed the moral light available to them, just as we read in Romans 1:18-19:

> The wrath of God is being revealed from heaven against all the godlessness and wickedness of men who suppress the truth by their wickedness, since what may be known about God is plain to them.

Although the language has the mind in view (understanding and ignorance), it must be remembered that biblical knowledge is far more than intellectual assent. It is a whole-life, obedient response to God. Conversely, ignorance is a failure to be grateful and obedient. We can only move from the latter to the former by the grace of God.

The consequence of such wilful disobedience is cumulative. Sensitivity is lost (v. 19) and there follows a self-destroying submission to a lifestyle which is utterly incompatible with Christian living. Those who are futile in their thinking, darkened in their understanding, ignorant and hard hearted, give themselves over to the vices of 'sensuality' and 'impurity', overwhelmed with a greedy, insatiable desire for sin. Ignorance and darkness of heart lead not only to a lack of moral sensitivity but also to an increasing desire for immorality. The depravity is absolute.

The greediness with which such sin is pursued relates to 'every kind of impurity'.

This is as shocking a picture of life without God as we have seen in 2:1-3 and 2:11-12. It is a very clear message, and very different from the common perceptions we have of humanity. However hard we try we will not be able to live the lives God wants for us unless firstly he has made us alive and secondly we are informed by his Word and obedient to it.

It is probably worth noting that this is not written *to* non-Christians. However, it is written *about* them. As such we may need to give a little time and thought to how we might deal with some of the inevitable questions which will be raised in the minds of those who hear these words. The description Paul gives of the average non-Christian is not one which most non-Christians would recognise. That was probably as true in the first century as it is in the twenty-first. The Gentiles living in Ephesus who came to faith in Christ would have been behaving in very similar ways to other non-Christian Gentiles before they heard the gospel. Within the framework of their society, their behaviour would have been quite normal and acceptable. In the same way, twenty-first century society dictates its own moral norms, usually by consensus opinion. The vast majority of people will happily live within this framework and will, therefore, rarely regard themselves as sinful. Only when someone steps outside that 'norm' is that behaviour regarded as wrong.

But we must remember that before God humanity is spiritually dead, unable to see the light of the gospel of the glory of Christ (2 Cor. 4:4; Eph. 2:1). Without the intervening grace of God and the convicting work of the

Spirit, sin will not be seen as sin and salvation from sin will not be understood. It is not that non-Christians are unable to decide what is right and wrong; it is simply that the non-Christians will have themselves set the parameters for what is right and wrong (the very problem for which Adam was evicted from the Garden of Eden and barred from the tree of life); they will play by their own rules. Sin will only be seen as that which transgresses the accepted moral code of the society rather than as a violation of God's holiness. Only when we see ourselves in comparison with the utter purity of God will we realise how degenerate we really are – and that will only happen by the gracious work of God. The reality is that all of us are capable of the most serious of sins. If the thoughts of our hearts were truly exposed to public view, even those who abide by the tribal rules of society would be revealed as utterly corrupt.

Paul is very keen that the Christians of Ephesus understand the contrast between the life they have been rescued from and the life they now have in Christ; the walk of the old man and the new. Ultimately it will be seen in right understanding of the God-given Word which leads to right living as God's new humanity.

You did not so learn Christ (4:20-24)

The dark warnings of 4:17-19 are now contrasted with the experience of the Ephesian Christians. The NIV does not convey the full impact of verse 20, which is better translated 'You did not so learn Christ.' The people of Ephesus were taught a different lifestyle as they heard the gospel of Christ.

Once again, the emphasis is on the mind. Just as futile, darkened and ignorant minds lead to debauchery, so informed and taught minds should lead to 'righteousness and holiness.' The teaching they heard and to which they responded relates directly to the historical person of Jesus, made clear by the fact that the only time in which the word 'Jesus' appears on its own is in verse 21. It is as if Paul wants to emphasise that the 'historical Jesus was the embodiment of the truth.'[2] They heard of him and were taught in him in accordance to the truth that is in Jesus.

In the Old Testament there is a very close connection between the given words of God and the voice of God. As Moses preached his final sermon before the people of God entered the Promised Land, he reminded them of their past experiences and prepared them for their future responsibilities. In looking back he took them to the foot of Mount Sinai where, with their own ears and with much trembling, they heard the voice of God (Deut. 5:23). This given Word was then recorded for later preaching with the expectation of obedient response. In the same way, therefore, as he looked forward to their future in the land, Moses reminded the people that as the given Word is preached, so they will hear the voice of God (Deut. 30:20), not 'audibly' but by the written Word.

In the same way, the New Testament apostolic teaching about Jesus which the Ephesians had been taught was the equivalent of 'hearing' the voice of Jesus. The original wording of verse 21 makes this link clear: 'you heard him and were taught by him' (my translation).

It means that authentic Christianity is far more than intellectual assent or even a simple profession of faith. Those who learnt Christ not only learned about him and how to live in order to please him, they were also responding directly to him in their day to day Christian living; there was a personal encounter with the living Christ. That encounter,

---

2   O'Brien, *Ephesians*, p. 326.

experienced in the teaching they received, involved putting off the old man (v. 22; NIV 'old self'), being made new (v. 23) and putting on the new man (v. 24; NIV 'new self'). Authentic faith always issues in authentic life-style change as a result of authentic encounter with the voice of the risen Lord Jesus. These three instructions are explained more fully in the following three verses.

Verse 22 reminds us that the old man, the 'former way of life,' which was ruled by sin and which was spiritually dead and alienated (2:1-3; 2:11-12) is being corrupted by deceitful desires. Unlike the truth which is in Christ (1:13; 4:15; 4:21; 5:9; 6:14), those dead in sin and in darkness are subject to deceit. The desires of sin promise so much and look so attractive, but they lead to death. The hidden deceit of sin is that it is presented to us with candy-coated allure. This lifestyle, the former conduct of the pre-Christian life, must be put away. What might look so attractive deceives us; it carries the stench of death and decay and leads to judgement. It corrupts and destroys.

Between discussion of the old man of verse 22 and the new man of verse 24 comes the instruction 'to be renewed in the spirit of your mind' (v. 23). Here the tense of the verb is different, suggesting that although this is a process which requires our mind, it comes from God. One of the strange paradoxes of the Christian walk is that although it is all our effort, it is also all from God. We walk in the ways God has prepared for us to walk in; we strive through obedience to do that which God will do and has done. We are to make ourselves new in mind, but God is the one who will bring about the transformation required. Such minds, renewed by the Spirit, are those which seek to understand the Word and be obedient to it. 'If heathen degradation is due to the futility of their minds, then Christian righteousness depends on the constant renewing of our minds.'[3]

The last verse of our section, verse 24, brings us to the third aspect of those who have learnt Christ. We are, literally, 'to put on the new man according to God created in righteousness and holiness of truth.' Although putting on the new self is a deliberate and active choice, this verse reminds us that the new creation is brought about by God himself (as 2:10). He is both the author of the new work and its model. As those redeemed and made new we should increasingly exhibit the God-like characteristics of the Lord Jesus Christ. He is the source of the truth from which they come. And as we obey his Word, as our minds are changed and informed, so our character should become more and more holy and righteous. As we grow up into him who is the head by being obedient to his Word we will grow into his likeness. The alternative is futile, darkened and ignorant thinking which leads to insatiable debauchery and results in death and judgement.

From text to teaching

The passage divides naturally into the two blocks of material which we have just studied, contrasting the life of the sinner and the life of the saint. Although we may preach this section as a unit, it is very much connected to what has gone before and it prepares us for what is yet to come. Here is Paul's conclusion to 4:1-16. The Word given, taught and obeyed enables us to become what we are, to grow into the unity, maturity and love for which we are to strive. This section is a great reminder of the folly and danger of the alternative position. In that sense it serves a different

---

3   Stott, *Ephesians*, p.182

purpose from the earlier reminders of what the Ephesians were before the Gospel came to them. Then Paul reminded them that they were dead in sin and alienated from one another. Now they are alive in Christ and made into a new people. These verses are not so much a contrast between the old and the new but rather a stern warning for those who have been made new not to return to the old ways. As such, our preaching must also contain an element of warning or urgency. Paul's double insistence and his reminder that this instruction is 'in the Lord' mean that we need to take this teaching very seriously indeed.

Introduction

We may need to include a reminder of what has gone before, especially if the congregation is likely to include a number of people who have not heard the previous section so that we do not lose the link that Paul has clearly made.

Many of us are likely to be blindly complacent about our Christian lives. It is very easy to start well and then to drift or to stop growing through limited Christian discipline or the lack of desire to be challenged. The dynamic nature of growth which is part and parcel of church (2:22; 4:15-16) requires us to be vigilant and diligent in our obedience to the Word. It is important that we capture the reality of this warning, explaining clearly the consequence of not responding rightly or of having uninformed minds. The introduction may serve to 'hook' the congregation by speaking directly into the situation in which we find ourselves, the very real lives of those to whom we are speaking.

Preaching outline – an example

There may not be much difference between the titles of the two sections. Our headings may vary, depending on our style and preference; we may prefer to use headings which are taken from the conclusion of each point so that people remember how the text is applied, or we may prefer to leave the headings as statements or warnings.

1.   4:17-19   Get your mind right: Don't live like a pagan

2.   4:20-24   Get your mind right: Remember what you heard.

Application

The very strong insistence of verse 17 provides us with the expected response to these words. Paul insists that those who hear Christ walk the right way – not as the Gentiles, uninformed, ignorant and sinful – but as those who have heard his voice and been made new.

It is unlikely that we will be speaking to congregations who are living lives of open debauchery and rebellion, but all of us need to examine our lives and consider how we are responding to God's Word. The two truths of the previous verses relating to the preaching of the Word and our response to it are grounded in the practical outworking of our daily lives. How we live is evidence of our relationship with Jesus, whatever we may look like or do on a Sunday morning. Before Paul begins to unpack how these verses are worked out in the various relationships which are part and parcel of our lives in the chapters that follow, this general pattern of behaviour should challenge our general mindset and the very real consequences of not submitting to the teaching of the Lord Jesus.

The evidence of a renewed mind is holy living. Therefore we must address the way in which our mind is being renewed and the way in which we are growing in holiness. This is a whole-life perspective relating to Christian character, the importance of which permeates the letter

(1:9-10; 2:7; 3:10). As the teaching is applied we should all be more determined to change our thinking in the light of the Bible in order that we might better walk the walk to which we have been called. We should also be aware that the alternative is not a neutral position but rather futile thinking and sinful living.

Questions for home groups/study groups

1. Who does Paul mean when he speaks here of the Gentiles (v. 17)?

2. What leads to wrong living?

3. Look carefully at what Paul tells us about the Gentiles – why have they got things wrong?

4. What does verse 19 tell us about the consequences of this error?

5. How does this section relate to 4:1-16?

6. How much does 4:17-19 resonate with your life?

7. In contrast, what were the Ephesian Christians taught?

8. What is the 'truth that is in Jesus' (v. 21)?

9. What is the problem with the 'old self'? What are you doing about this?

10. How are we to be 'made new in the attitude of our minds'? (Note 4:1-16)

11. What are the characteristics of the 'new self'?

12. What has Paul already told us about how we do this?

13. What might we have to do differently in the light of these verses?

9

RELATIONSHIPS IN THE CHURCH:
BE LIKE GOD (4:25–5:2)

For many of us church is what we do on a Sunday morning. The idea that our new identity should be worked out in every area of our lives is something which we often know in our heads but have less experience of in our daily living. And yet throughout Ephesians we are presented with an extraordinarily high doctrine of the church. When rightly living, we are a picture of what God is doing in eternity, an example of where history is heading; a foretaste of the future which causes Satan to shudder. The way in which we relate to one another and as God's people to the world is a practical outworking of what it means to be church. As we have seen, it can only happen when the Word is rightly obeyed, when we live as the 'new man' in holiness and righteousness, and when we serve one another in works of ministry. This is the Christian 'walk' to which we are called not only individually but together as God's people. We must walk this way not only on a Sunday morning, but in every area of our lives.

In the remaining chapters of Ephesians, church life is worked out in three main areas of relationship. In some ways the distinctions are blurred, but as we study each section we shall see why and how they are divided into these areas. The first is in our relationships within the church (4:25–5:2). The second is in the relationship of the church with the world (5:3-14) and the third is in the relationships within the domestic sphere (wives and husbands, children and parents, slaves and masters) (5:22–6:9). In between the second and third areas there is a summary and linking section (5:15-21) which serves not only as a conclusion to the first two but also as a preparation for the third.

Preliminary observations

This section is about how we live together within the body of Christ as 'members of one body.' At the end of the previous section we were encouraged to live 'like God' (NIV – i.e., according to the character of God) in true righteousness and holiness (4:24). At the end of this section we are encouraged to 'be imitators of God' (5:1). The two 'therefores' (4:25 and 5:1) provide the bookends to secure the unit. This is all about how we behave as the 'new man' within our church relationships.

As with many writers of the time, Paul supplies us with a catalogue of virtues and vices. The virtues relate to the outworking of the new man, empowered and indwelt by the Spirit, and the vices to the outworking of the old. In that sense, they all relate to the previous section.

Listening to the text

(25) Therefore, each of you must put off falsehood and speak truthfully to his neighbour, for we are all members

of one body. (26) 'In your anger do not sin': Do not let the sun go down while you are still angry, (27) and do not give the devil a foothold. (28) He who has been stealing must steal no longer, but must work, doing something useful with his own hands, that he may have something to share with those in need. (29) Do not let any unwholesome talk come out of your mouths, but only what is helpful for building up others according to their needs, that it may benefit those who listen. (30) And do not grieve the Holy Spirit of God, with whom were you were sealed for the day of redemption. (31) Get rid of all bitterness, rage and anger, brawling and slander, along with every form of malice. (32) Be kind and compassionate to one another, forgiving each other, just as in Christ God forgave you. (5:1) Be imitators of God, therefore, as dearly loved children (2) and live a life of love, just as Christ loved us and gave himself up for us as a fragrant offering and sacrifice to God.

Don't give the devil a foothold (4:25-28)
Lies, anger and theft are all marks of the old man, characteristic of those in whom the Lord has not been at work. As Paul begins to deal with what of the old man must be removed, it is these three vices to which he turns.

Speak the truth (4:25)
We have already seen in this chapter that truth is found in Jesus (4:21) and comes from God (4:24). It should characterise the way in which we relate to one another if the church is to be built into the maturity and unity that has been won for us in Christ (4:15-16). However, there may be even greater significance to Paul's choice of words. The phrase 'Speak the truth to each other' comes directly from Zechariah 8:16, which occurs within a passage (8:16-19)

which follows God's promises about the New Jerusalem (8:1-15). The remnant of God's people will inhabit Zion. The fact that this is now directed to the new people of God, who have been made into one body (1:23; 2:16; 4:4, 12, 15, 16), shows the significance and importance of right behaviour for the church, God's New Testament people. Speaking truthfully to one another is a sign that we are part of the new community of God's people, anticipated in the Old Testament but now made known to us through the apostles and prophets. Our truthfulness to one another marks us out as part of God's new end-times community.

Be angry but don't sin (4:26-27)

Here again Paul cites the Old Testament. In Psalm 4 the psalmist is perturbed by false accusations but, as he cries to God, his anger is replaced with a heart of joy and peace. This work of God-given peace is a mark of what it means to be a part of God's new people, foreshadowed in the experience of the psalmist.

The NIV has probably got the feel of the phrase about right ('in your anger do not sin'). The original seems slightly more difficult to understand: 'Be angry and do not sin'. It suggests that anger is permitted, although it must be different from the anger of verse 31, which is condemned. Presumably then, anger can be righteous and holy (v. 24). But before we breathe a sigh of relief or justify our actions after an elders' meeting, we need to heed the warnings or prohibitions, of which there are three:

+ Don't sin

+ Don't continue after sunset

+ Don't give the devil a foothold

Most of our anger is rarely righteous and holy and, even when it is, we should not let it fester. It should be over before the evening meeting. We would be wise to be very cautious here. Our sinful self-righteousness is likely to lead us to the 'subtle temptation to regard my anger as righteous indignation and other people's anger as sheer bad temper.'[1] It is better to assume that our anger is unrighteous than to clothe it in the folly of self-righteousness. Such pious wrapping of the old man is perhaps the most distasteful and spiritually damaging of all.

Note that there is no suggestion that anger is caused by the devil. It does, though, give him a chance to disrupt that which God has created. Here we come across an important yet relatively understated theme in the letter. Satan is mentioned twice in Ephesians before we get to the passage in chapter 6 about spiritual warfare (although he is described in different ways). The first, which occurs in 2:2, reminds us that before we come to faith in Christ we are under his authority. The second is found in these verses, which presumably relates not only to anger but to all the vices listed in this passage (lying (25), stealing (28) and unwholesome talk (29)). Satan does not want people to become Christians and he does not want people to live as Christians. It means that we give him a foothold when, in our relationships, we live in ways which do not reflect the new man. Our anger, falsehood and lack of love provide what the devil needs to climb all over the church. One of the reasons relationships can be so difficult in church is that Satan targets them. He seeks to undermine that which God has created.

---

1   O'Brien, *Ephesians*, p. 340, quoting F.F. Bruce, *Ephesians*.

When we begin to unpack how this relates to the letter to the Ephesians and to the Bible as a whole, the activity of Satan becomes clear. He does not want the sinner to be redeemed (making evangelism difficult); he does not want the Word preached (making faithful, accurate Bible teaching a spiritual challenge) and he does not want those who have been redeemed to live as God's people (making church relationships strained).

But when the church lives as the church, Satan knows his days are numbered (3:10); we become a picture of his defeat. No wonder he is so concerned to attack the church (in our relationships) and to distort that which can grow the church (by twisting the given Word). It is the Word rightly obeyed, issuing in acts of ministry, by which the church is built. As we respond with Spirit-renewed minds so we are enabled to grow in love, truth, unity and maturity. Of course, the Lord Jesus is of infinitely greater power than the devil (as we shall see more clearly in chapter 6); nevertheless, we need to be aware of how Satan works and to realise that it will be in the everyday relationships with other Christians that the rot sets in. When we are tempted to be unloving, unkind or impatient, when we do not bear with one another in love or when we talk about others behind their backs, or tear them down (even if we pretend our motive is Christian), we give the devil a foothold. The spiritual warfare in which we are engaged is simply to be the church. Our battle against the spiritual forces of evil in the heavenly realms (6:12) is the battle to avoid getting angry, to speak truthfully and helpfully, to build up and not to tear down; in short, it is the battle to love as Christ loves, for that, above all, marks us out as disciples. It is in the day to day relationships with other Christians that this battle is fought.

Don't steal but do good (4:28)
There is clear injunction against stealing in the Old
Testament. The fact that it is mentioned here suggests
not simply that it was a problem in the Ephesian church,
but also, particularly if it was a circular letter, that it was
a general problem. Without a welfare state, many people
before becoming Christians would steal. It was probably
much more acceptable behaviour and may even have carried
on once people came to faith in Christ. But that was the
old man. The new man is different. In contrast to stealing –
which can only harm others – the new man is to work (the
Word suggests to the point of weariness) in order that it
might be possible to help those in need.

Don't grieve the Holy Spirit (4:29-32)
As we move into 4:29 from the three warnings relating to
lies, anger and theft, Paul appears to return to the original
subject of speech (as 4:25). If the earlier verse has told us
what to do (speaking the truth in love), the latter verse
explains the desired outcome of what we do (that others
may be built up according to their needs).

In that sense, this instruction flows from 4:28 where
believers are to seek the good of others. And just as people
are to do good with their hands (4:28), so also they are to
do good with their lips (4:29). Both relate to the 'truthing in
love' of 4:15 and both are essential for the good and growth
of the church. We need to help others and build them up,
in our actions and our speech. Obedient Christians should
always have a concern for the good and growth of their
brothers and sisters in Christ.

The motivation for this behaviour comes in 4:30 (hence
the 'and' linking the verses). It is that we should not grieve
the Holy Spirit. This instruction parallels the advice about

not giving the devil a foothold and may well be placed here so as to offer a contrast. The devil may be powerful and may try to disrupt, but the Spirit, working within the church, is greater. He triumphs over the evil one. For this reason I have subtitled the two sections under these two headings, *'Don't give the devil a foothold'* and *'Don't grieve the Holy Spirit'.*

'The Holy Spirit of God' is an unusual term, but a link to Isaiah 63 could explain it. There we are reminded of the Exodus and of Yahweh, who redeemed his people from Egypt and led them by his personal presence (the Holy Spirit, Isaiah 63:10). In Ephesians 4:30 this same idea is applied to the new people of God (Jew and Gentile). These people have been sealed by the Spirit (1:13), made into a new people (2:14-18) and indwelt by the Spirit (2:21-22; 4:3-4). Paul applies the truth of the people of God in the Old Testament to the new people of God in the New Testament. The Holy Spirit of God has made and leads a new people from the redemption at Calvary, from which they have every blessing in Christ, to the full redemption of 1:10, when God will bring all things together in heaven and on earth under one head, even Christ. We have been sealed for that day (1:10, 14; 2:7; 5:5; 6:8, 13), but the effect of that is seen in the church now (3:10).

The church, therefore, as God's new community, is the place where we see what has been achieved in the heavenly realms, in Christ, displayed on earth. Behaving in ways which are inconsistent with this grieves the Spirit who lives within the growing church. And so we see that the devil seeks to undermine that which God has created, but the Spirit builds that which God has created. Just as wrong words (lies, slander, anger, rage, malice, unwholesome talk, slander etc.) and wrong actions (stealing etc.) tear down, so right actions and right words build up. One is of the old man and the other is of the new man. One is the activity of Satan and the other the activity of the Spirit – but, as the order here shows, the Spirit trumps Satan. We must not live in ways which fail to show that he is at work within us.

Ephesians 4:31-32 may well be a continuation of this theme (i.e. this is how we live in a way which does not grieve the Spirit), but perhaps this also serves as a summary. We are given a comprehensive list which starts on the inside and works to the outside: bitterness, rage and anger are all, initially, personal and internal; brawling and slander[2] are both verbal and outwards. This results in every kind of malice. But in contrast, the new man, empowered by the Spirit, will be kind, compassionate and forgiving (4:32). The motivation and model for this right living are what God has done in Christ. It is, therefore, the content of what we have already seen in chapters 1-3. As we understand what Christ has done and what God is now doing in us through his Spirit, so we are motivated to live in right ways.

Conclusion: Be imitators of God (5:1-2)

The instruction in 4:24 that the new man is 'created to be like God' finds an echo in these verses which suggests that 4:25–5:2 is a unit, all of which relates to our relationships within the church. We are to be like God, to imitate him as those who have been adopted into his family, as his dearly loved children. This is the only place in the New Testament where believers are asked to be imitators of God. In many ways, of course, that is impossible. He is the creator and we are the created, but in the specific ways mentioned here it is

---

2   Slander is a translation of the word 'blasphemy' which was used in non-Biblical language for abusive speech.

both possible (because the Spirit is at work) and expected (because God commands it).

We are to be imitators of him both in our attitude of forgiveness within the church (4:32), and in our sacrificial love (5:2). We are to live a life of love; or, more accurately, we are to walk in love. Both aspects of our living are therefore to be modelled on the cross. God forgave us in Christ, and so we should be forgiving; Jesus gave his life for us in love as a fragrant offering and sacrifice to God, and so too we should be loving, giving our lives to others. This is pleasing to God; this is the life of the new man, empowered by the Spirit, like God in our forgiveness and like Jesus in our love. What is more, we know from the chapters already studied that God has done everything to make this possible. We have every spiritual blessing in Christ, we have been raised with him to the heavenly realms, we are being built together to become a dwelling in which God lives by his Spirit, we have been given the unity of the Spirit (4:3) and we have been told how we become what we are. It means that this kind of living, this 'walk,' is not impossible. It is the normal life of the church, or should be.

From text to teaching

As we preach this passage we need to be conscious of two misunderstandings which may well be in the minds of those to whom we are speaking. The first relates to the confusion between the sovereignty of God and the responsibility of his people. Many of us have been taught that our Christian lives are lived in response to his love and that the ethical instruction in the New Testament is no more than a list of how we should live in order to please him as a response to his gracious initiative. Whilst there is truth in this assertion, it can lead to unhealthy and unhelpful polarisation between his work and ours. Our studies in Ephesians will have made it clear that God has given us everything in Christ and he has already prepared good works for us to walk in. The unity of the Spirit has already been created through the work of Jesus. These instructions are about how we live out what we are and become what God has made us. And whilst we have to make an effort with our words and our actions, it is all his work. Contrary to what many may think, the evidence that *God* is at work in us by his Spirit is that *we* will make every effort to walk his way. In that sense the Bible holds together what we often polarise. It is all God's work but it is seen in our personal effort to live for him. If we polarise these truths the result is either guilt or apathy, or both.

The second misunderstanding relates to our experience of spiritual warfare. Not until chapter 6 will Paul unpack all that it means and how we fight this fight, but we need to be aware as we preach 4:27 and the surrounding verses that many will not associate spiritual warfare with the day to day reality of church relationships. Gossip, slander, back-biting, cliques, complaints and grumbles are all too readily accepted as part and parcel of church life – but all show the work both of our sin (which is dealt with on the cross) and of Satan (who is defeated on the cross and over whom the risen Lord Jesus has authority). The devil seeks to undermine that which God has created. That will be seen in the conversations over coffee at the end of the service, the Christian slander and gossip, often falsely clothed in the language 'just so you can pray', all of which will be of great potential damage to the church. The relationships we have with one another as Christians are of great spiritual significance and will be the target for spiritual warfare. We must not underestimate the nature of this battle.

Introduction

Any sermon introduction to this material will need to 'hook' the attention of the congregation. A challenge to the complacency about our church relationships or a description of what church life is really like will helpfully unsettle many of us who profess faith in Christ. Most of us do not live as God's people are expected to live and most of us will not know why it is so difficult or why it is so important. If we are to respond rightly to the challenge of these verses we will first need to see that in many cases we are simply not doing what God requires. A powerful introduction might include the very real experiences of church life, the gossip and the slander, the hurt and the pain; and the very real questions these raise in the minds of those who expect the church to be loving and kind.

Preaching outline – an example

1. Don't give the devil a foothold   4:25-28

2. Don't grieve the Holy Spirit   4:29-31

3. Be imitators of God   5:1-2

Application

These words are applying the gospel truths of the first two chapters in the day to day reality of church life. For those to whom we preach it is all too easy to assume that they relate either to unique problems in Ephesus or that they are applicable to churches with particular problems of gossip or bitterness, anger or stealing. But these are not simply words for other people; they are words for us. As those who are 'created to be like God' and instructed to 'be imitators of God', we need to ensure that the light of God's Word penetrates deeply into our hard hearts.

If we have used the introduction to challenge the assumptions of what is acceptable in our own church practice, then our application must encourage us to change. The congregation needs to leave the church gathering thinking about what we can do in order to share with those in need (especially within the congregation), how we can speak to one another in order to build people up, how we can show kindness, love and compassion. There needs to be an active challenge to stop some of the more acceptable sins of church life and to live differently.

Questions for home groups/study groups

1. Look at the two 'therefores' of 4:25 and 5:1. What do they relate to and what do they tell us about Christian living?

2. Read Zechariah 8:1-15, 16-19. Who are the people here who are to speak truth? Why might this be significant for our understanding of Ephesians? How might this relate to being members of one body (See also 4:15, 16, 21, 24)?

3. Read Psalm 4. What is the experience of the Psalmist? What does this tell us about right living? What is the difference between the anger of 4:26 and that of 4:31? When, if ever, is anger righteous and holy? Are there any exceptions to controlling righteous anger? If so, what?

4. When is the devil given a foothold? How do you see that in your local church?

5. What must we do with our hands and our lips? In what sense does 4:28-29 describe you? In the light of these verses, what do you need to do differently? Where do you need to repent?

6. How do we grieve the Holy Spirit? Why do you think Paul specifically mentions the day of redemption? Why is this important for the church?

7. What are the two models given here for right Christian living?

8. What of the 'old man' do you need to remove? What of the 'new man' do you need to adopt?

9. How does this passage affect your understanding of what it means to be church?

10

RELATIONSHIPS WITH THE WORLD: BE LIGHT (5:3-14)

It is often said that character is what you are when you are on your own. For Christians there must be no distinction between the public and the private or between our life with other Christians and our life with non-Christians. The integrity of character and godliness of living which is possible because of the grace of God must be manifest in all situations; and when it comes to our relationship with the world we need to be both distinct from it and a witness to it. And so in these words Paul turns to our relationship with the world, beginning with the necessity to be distinct from the world and its values (in our living and our language) and the necessity to engage with the world (in terms of living as light).

We would do well to spend time thinking through the implications of this passage, especially as many of us live in an environment where we hear the subtle messages that certain forms of immorality, impurity and greed are acceptable. We need to see the severity and significance of these words in relation to what we have been made in Christ. This is what the church in the world is meant to look like, as an outcrop of eternity (picturing 1:10) and as a manifestation of the wisdom of God to the rulers and authorities in the heavenly realms (3:10)

Preliminary observations

Not all commentators would take this section as one unit, but there does seem to be something of a shift in Paul's focus between 4:25–5:2 and 5:3-14. Unlike the previous section, which focused on temptations that face us inside the church, this section deals with sexual purity – and the challenges to that come mainly from outside the church. The pagans of Ephesus, steeped as they were in the cult of Artemis and the sexual rituals that often went with it, would have found the distinct living of the Christian Ephesians strange and would not have shared any of their moral qualms about their sexual behaviour.

These people seem to be in Paul's mind as he writes 5:6-7. It is the empty words of the sons of disobedience which are a threat to the church. The challenge for Christians, then as now, as they and we engage in the world and live our lives in a very different moral climate from the world around us is this: influence or be influenced. Such is the concern here in this contrast between believers and sinful outsiders.

Listening to the text

(3) But among you there must not be even a hint of sexual immorality, or of any kind of impurity, or of greed, because these are improper for God's holy people. (4) Nor should there be obscenity, foolish talk or coarse joking, which are out of place, but rather thanksgiving. (5) For of this you can be sure: No immoral, impure or greedy person – such

a man is an idolater – has any inheritance in the kingdom of Christ and of God. (6) Let no-one deceive you with empty words, for because of such things God's wrath comes on those who are disobedient. (7) Therefore do not be partners with them.

(8) For you were once darkness, but now you are light in the Lord. Live as children of light (9) (for the fruit of light consists in all goodness, righteousness and truth) (10) and find out what pleases the Lord. (11) Have nothing to do with the fruitless deeds of darkness, but rather expose them. (12) For it is shameful even to mention what the disobedient do in secret. (13) But everything exposed by the light becomes visible, (14) for it is light makes everything visible. This is why it is said:

'Wake up, O sleeper,
Rise from the dead,
And Christ will shine on you.'

The text naturally falls into two sections, the first of which is a warning about the immorality around and the second a reminder of how to be light in a dark world. These two sections naturally lead to two points in a sermon.

Let no-one deceive you: warnings about immorality and greed (5:3-7)

This section begins (5:3) with a warning against the opposite of sacrificial love. Having just encouraged the Ephesians to live lives of love modelled on Christ they must be very careful to avoid the self-indulgent behaviour of those around them. As with many similar passages, sexual immorality heads the list (cf. 1 Cor. 6:9, 18; Gal. 5:19; Col. 3:5). No authentic Christian should act like this. Sexual immorality is incompatible with authentic Christian living, whatever the world around may say.

The word used for '*sexual immorality*' (porneia) is a term which 'denotes any kind of sexual intercourse especially adultery and sexual relations with prostitutes'[1]. Later literature suggests that this might include any kind of extramarital or unnatural sexual intercourse. Although the word which follows, '*impurity*', is often associated with sexual immorality here the addition of the words 'any kind' suggests more than this. Paul has in mind anything which is unholy. The last of the three words is '*greed*' which also was often associated with immorality in the ancient world. The greedy man wants more, whether it is possessions or sex. Any form of greed places a person, item or desire as the object of affection and worship and is therefore idolatry. So serious is this that we, as believers, should avoid thinking and talking about them. Character is indeed what we are when we are on our own – even in our thoughts.

Paul's list of vices continues in verse 4 but he moves from sexual attitudes to ungodly speech. The words are unique to this passage, found nowhere else in the New Testament, and it is likely that they all relate to verbalising the sexual immorality which is condemned in the previous verse. Non-Christians may debase sex and engage in smutty language, but in contrast that which comes from the lips of Christians must be of an entirely different character.[2]

In contrast we are to recognise God's generosity and to be thankful. Our language should not, therefore, be about what we can take, but be full of thankfulness for that which we have received. 'Thanksgiving is almost a synonym for the Christian life; it is the response of gratitude to God's saving

---

1   O'Brien, *Ephesians*, p. 359.
2   Foulkes, *Ephesians*, describes some of the language in this way 'All that is shameless, all that would make a morally sensitive person ashamed', p. 147.

activity in creation and redemption and thus a recognition that he is the ultimate source of every blessing.'[3] In fact, thanksgiving is one of the marks of being made alive in Christ. It is a mark of the Spirit, a consequence of being a recipient of God's unmerited kindness and being made a part of the new people of God (as in 5:18-20).

Verse 5 brings the first of two warnings. If Christians live like this (immoral, impure or greedy) without repentance and shame, they do not have an inheritance in the kingdom. Here Paul deliberately uses the present tense. Those who unrepentantly live this way have (in the present) no inheritance. He may be hinting at the nature of the kingdom, described here rather unusually as 'the kingdom of Christ and of God.' Often in Paul's writing the kingdom of God refers to his future activity and the kingdom of Christ refers to his present activity. The inclusion of both may suggest both present and future reality of the church. We are a picture of what is yet to come; and if we do not live out what we are, then both the present reality of the kingdom, manifest in the people of God, and the future promises are forfeited.

The second warning comes in verse 6. Just as the 'Christian' who is repeatedly and unrepentantly sexually immoral has no inheritance in the present, so also the wrath of God is experienced (present tense) by those who are disobedient. No doubt, just as today, the pagan mind obviously did not think that these practices were a problem and may even have thought it rather strange that Christians behaved differently. It would have been very easy to have been deceived by their words. The only solution? Do not be partners with them: think, speak and act differently.

---

3   O'Brien, *Ephesians*, p.361.

Walk as children of light (5:8-14)

Paul now moves to a contrast between dark and light which runs throughout these verses. The Ephesian Christians have undergone a huge change; they have moved from darkness to light. As a result they must now live appropriately in the world.

Having given the negative consequences of not living rightly, Paul now gives the positive reasons (v. 8). There has been a cosmic change in the lives of the Ephesians. It was not simply that they once lived in darkness (although that is true); they *were* darkness and *are now* light. It is therefore their lives and not their surroundings which have changed. They still live in the pagan culture of Ephesus but rather than being part of it they are now to be distinct from it. This change from darkness to light necessitates a new walk as children of light which is described (v. 9) as goodness, righteousness and truth. All of these are ideas we have come across already (2:10; 4:24; 4:15, 21, 25) and all relate to the character of God. In contrast to the unfruitful deeds of darkness (v. 11), Christians are to live like God.

That will involve (v. 10) finding out what pleases the Lord, which is not so much working out something which has not yet been made known but rather coming to understand how to live in the light of that which has already been revealed. They have already 'learned Christ' (4:21). They were taught how to live. Now they must live that out in the cosmopolitan and worldly city of Ephesus.

That, of course, does not mean to withdraw from the world. Although they are told to 'have nothing to do with the fruitless deeds of darkness' (v. 11a), that does not mean that they should build a monastery or withdraw into a sub-cultural Christian ghetto. It would be impossible to fulfil the second half of the verse ('but rather expose them.' v. 11b) without living in the world alongside those who are in darkness.

As that happens, sinful deeds (rather than the sinner) are exposed, in part at least by the contrast with Christian lives. Just as pure white reveals more clearly the impurity of colours placed next to it, so Christian living highlights the sin of the world. It is godly engagement, not religious withdrawal which is required, even though we must be careful not even to 'mention what the disobedient do in secret' (v. 12).

Verses 13 and 14 have caused a little more debate, but, rightly understood, seem to be consistent with what we have just read. We are told, literally, that 'everything exposed is light'. This suggests that the darkness in which the Ephesians live becomes light as they live as children of light within it. Some have suggested alternative meanings, assuming that the light must be referring to that which shines on believers, with the underlying assumption that they are not living in the right ways (because of the influence of the world) and therefore need to wake up and change. Indeed, the phrase is thought by some to be an early Christian hymn fragment which Paul included to remind the Ephesians of their baptism and the promises made to them and by them.

But it seems unlikely that it applies to the current lives of believers. Even though Paul has encouraged the Ephesians not to live as the Gentiles do, who are darkened in their understanding, in the futility of their thinking (4:17-18), they were taught something different. They are now light, the gospel has already taken root in their lives (1:15-16). They may need to grow and live wisely, but they can hardly be described as dead.

Whether the fragment was used for baptism or not may not be particularly relevant. It might be possible that Paul is reminding them of their calling, but more importantly we should remember that they too were once darkness. Now they are light. In the same way as those who are light exhibit the fruit of light, they not only expose darkness but also attract people to the light. True, some will prefer darkness because their deeds are evil (as John 3:19-20) but others will be attracted by the light, will repent and respond to the gospel (as 2 Cor. 4:6; Matt. 5:16). If that is the case, then the fragment (which may also have echoes of Isa. 29:18 and 60:1-2) would not only be a reminder of what happened to the Ephesians and therefore an encouragement to live rightly, but also a reminder of what can happen to those in darkness. They may yet become Christians.

So we need to be encouraged. We are not only to live rightly in the midst of darkness and thereby to expose the reality of godless lives, but by doing so those very lives may be changed. The testimony of many, if not most Christians, is that it was the lives of other believers which first attracted them to the Christian faith: love for one another and godly living in a dark world; holding on to and holding out the Word of life in a crooked and depraved generation. The challenge, therefore, is to influence the world by living rightly within it; the alternative is to be influenced by it.

Linking to the next section
In many ways these verses are a link between this section and the next. They remind us to live rightly by including three contrasts: not unwise but wise, not foolish but according to the Lord's will and not getting drunk but being filled with the Spirit. While the first and the second of these fit as a natural conclusion to the section we have just studied,

the third reminds us what a Spirit-filled Christian looks like. The areas covered include our living as Christians, our on-going thankfulness (presumably in all situations) and the way in which the church operates in the domestic relationships of wives and husbands, children and parents, and slaves and masters.

If we have time within a sermon series we might take 5:15-20 (or v. 21) as a separate section. Alternatively we could use it as a conclusion to this sermon and an introduction to the next. The holistic nature of what it contains means that it sums up much of which we read in the 'ethical' section of the letter. However, it requires some careful attention. The wording, the paragraph break and the subtitle of the NIV, which many of us will be using, do not help to make the passage as clear as they might, as we will see in the next chapter.

From text to teaching

The division in the passage lends itself naturally to two sermon points, but within each point there are clear sub-points.

Introduction

The challenge in these words is directly related to how we live as Christians within the world. There are perhaps two points of contact which we might consider using in our introduction: the first relates to the 'hint' of sexual immorality, any kind of impurity or greed. If we are honest, many Christians appear quite happy with the concept of a 'hint' of sin. As long as we do not indulge in too much sexual immorality, too much impurity or too much greed, all will be well. Or so we think. But here we are reminded (as we discover in the Sermon on the Mount) that even the smallest suggestion of immoral, impure or greedy behaviour should be of concern to us. An introduction which picks up what we really think and then brings our hearers to these words could prove very arresting.

The second possible point of contact relates to our partnership with the world. All of us engage in the world around us in a host of different ways. We are immersed in the messages of our culture and the mindset of our colleagues; we are party to the gossip of the world. But we are to have 'nothing to do with the fruitless deeds of darkness.' The very real challenge of how we live as Christians in the world, grounded in the experience of our hearers, might serve to draw attention to the teaching of this passage and link well to the application and conclusion of the sermon.

Preaching outline – an example

1. 5:3-7   Let no-one deceive you
      + Watch your living
      + Watch your language

2. 5:8-10   Live as children of light

3. 5:11-14   Expose the darkness

The following headings might be a little more cryptic but perhaps also more engaging.

1. 5:3-7   Watch out for the darkness
      + It will destroy you

2. 5:8-14   Walk as children of light
      + It will save those around you

Application

As we preach we need to be aware that these issues are far more real for people than many would like to admit. Even those who have outwardly happy and godly marriages may battle with unhealthy thoughts or pornographic pursuits. Those who are single may also find it very difficult to be distinct from the prevailing sexualised culture around them. Impurity in our thinking, our language and our daily living, in which we subtly compromise righteous living, is for many very difficult to avoid. The value system of the world around us is very different from that which is generated by the gospel, but the world will see nothing wrong with such values. As a result, the 'empty words' which deceive us can appear very 'normal' and the temptation to partner with the world no more than what normal people do. It is therefore only as we understand what we are in Christ and how we live as God's new humanity that we can begin to relate to the world around us in truly godly ways. There must not be so much as a hint of wrong behaviour as we live as Christians in the world.

These are very challenging words when applied to the daily living of the congregation to whom we preach. How we behave with our work colleagues, our non-Christian friends and those we deal with outside church, is part of what it means to be Christian, to be light in the world.

Likewise we need to remember that most effective evangelism is long-term, low-key and relational. Jesus expects those around us to see our Christian lives (Matt. 5:16); Peter expects persecuted Christians not only to be able to explain their faith but to have exemplary lives, so that those who 'speak maliciously against your good behaviour in Christ may be ashamed of their slander' (1 Pet. 3:16). We must live wisely in the world; not withdrawing from it, but being light within it. As we do so, those who are spiritually dead may 'wake up' as Christ shines on them (5:14).

Questions for home groups/study groups

1. A question for personal contemplation: Do you ever have any sexually immoral or impure thoughts? If so, what would the apostle Paul say to you (5:3-7)?

2. Think back to what you have said over the last week. How does your language compare with the list of prohibitions in verse 4?

3. What is the right alternative to these thoughts and words?

4. Why is this so significant?

5. Practically speaking, how are we to avoid being 'partners' with the world without withdrawing from it?

6. How do you know whether you are light or darkness (v. 8)?

7. What does it mean to 'find out what pleases the Lord' (given what we have already seen in 4:21-24)?

8. According to verses 11-13, how do we expose the 'fruitless deeds of darkness'?

9. As well as light exposing darkness, what else can happen (5:8, 13, 14)?

10. How should we live in the world?

11. Where do you need to change?

11

RELATIONSHIPS WITH EACH OTHER:
BE CAREFUL (5:15-21)

The implications of what it means to be Spirit-filled are often vigorously debated in churches. It is all too easy to read verses in isolation and to create a theology removed from context, sometimes with damaging and hurtful consequences. Such is the danger of this small section from Ephesians 5. The infilling of the Spirit, the contrast with drunkenness and even the mention of 'spiritual songs' can lead us to a theology which is not sustained by the rest of the letter and which, if wrongly understood, can lead to the kind of divisions which are in direct opposition to the content of the book. Yet when rightly understood these verses not only challenge our understanding of what it means to be a Spirit-filled Christian but also explain what it means to live as Spirit-filled believers within the church.

Preliminary observations

It is not usually very wise to start a sermon with a passage which concludes what has gone before. These verses are unashamedly part of the flow of Paul's argument from 4:1 to

6:9 which will inevitably have to be broken up into distinct preaching units if they are to be rightly understood and digested. Where we make our divisions will be determined, in large part, by our context, but these verses are so rich in content and so easily misunderstood that it may be wise to take them as a unit on their own.

In doing so we must not forget that they form not only a conclusion to the preceding sections but also prepare us for the lengthy and important teaching about household relationships. All this ethical teaching is an outworking of what it means to be a part of God's new people, the church. It all relates to becoming what we are as we obey the given and taught Word. There will be a need for constant and sensitive reminders that none of the material in the second half of the letter should be separated from what we have been told about what we are in the first half of the letter.

Just as it might be a little strange to start at verse 15, so it is perhaps also strange to conclude at verse 21. Although the NIV makes a distinction between this verse and the next, the discussion of submission in verse 21 is carried on (without another verb) into verse 22, as well as being a part of the preceding discussion of what it means to be a Spirit-filled Christian. Before preaching any section in these chapters we need to study them carefully and decide how to divide them up only when we understand what they are saying.

These verses have often been regarded as the 'summary climax' of the ethical section because they contain what appears to be general information about Christian relationships. The nature of the language has also led some to suggest that this must have the church's corporate worship in view (psalms, hymns and spiritual songs) and whilst thought of the church gathering must be included, the scope of the instruction carries far beyond our set gatherings and penetrates deeply into our everyday lives, as the household instructions which follow make clear.

The section begins by reminding Christians to be very careful about their 'walk' (NIV 'how you live'). By now we will recognise that this is the major concern of these final chapters: Ephesians 4:1–6:9 is all about our Christian 'walk'. We have been called and equipped to walk a different way, as the new man: a walk which demonstrates the future in the present and manifests God's wisdom to the rulers and authorities in the heavenly realms. Verse 15 contains the final reminder about this 'walk' and sets us up for the verses that follow, right through to 6:9. Whilst 5:15–6:9 is therefore a natural unit, it may be too much to tackle in one bite.

Listening to the text

> (15) Be very careful, then, how you live – not as unwise but as wise, (16) making the most of every opportunity, because the days are evil. (17) Therefore do not be foolish, but understand what the Lord's will is. (18) Do not get drunk on wine, which leads to debauchery. Instead, be filled with the Spirit. (19) Speak to one another with psalms, hymns and spiritual songs. Sing and make music in your heart to the Lord, (20) always giving thanks to God for everything, in the name of our Lord Jesus Christ. (21) Submit to one another out of reverence for Christ.

The three contrasts which emerge in these verses (wise/unwise, foolish/understanding, drunkenness/Spirit-filling) may provide a useful sermon structure, especially if the unit is to be preached either in association with what has gone before, or as part of 5:15–6:9, but there is so much within the third contrast (5:18-21) that it may be more advisable to divide the talk into two, looking first at 5:15-17 and then 5:18-21. If time allows and the congregation is able to take it, 5:18-21 could even be preached as a stand-alone sermon, although the link between what comes before and after would need careful attention.

Wise living (5:15-17)

The first of the three contrasts follows the headline statement 'Be very careful then how you live' (v. 15). Although we need to be careful not to give the impression that you need to read the text in Greek to understand it, it is important to recognise that here we have Paul's final mention of our 'walk': we need to be 'careful how we walk'. What is useful about the NIV translation is that our walk does affect our whole lives; yet, its choice of words loses the contrast between the old walk of 2:2 and the new walk of 2:10, a contrast which has been critical for our understanding of what has been taught throughout chapters 4 and 5.

The contrast of 5:15 relates to wisdom and the lack of wisdom. It is good to remember that wisdom has already been lavished upon us through the redemption that came by God's grace (1:8-9) and that Paul has already prayed for believers that they and we might know God better through that same wisdom (1:17-19). His prayer is for us to know what we already have in Christ, which, when we understand it, we will live out in the church. We therefore become the manifestation of God's wisdom (3:10). So wise living is living as the church, which will be seen in our relationships with God and with one another; the two relationships which have been brought about by the gospel and are seen in the church (2:1-22). That will involve 'making the most of every opportunity' (v. 16: literally, 'redeeming the time') because the days in which we live are evil. Here then is a picture of the church living as light in a dark world, demonstrating the future in the present and manifesting the power and wisdom of God.

The second contrast is between foolishness and understanding (v. 17). Folly has a great biblical history and almost always relates to a failure to understand what God wants for his people; a failure to do his will. Fortunately for us that will has already been revealed. Paul became an apostle by the will of God (1:1); a people of God was predestined through the will of God (1:5); his revealed will is ultimately for all things in heaven and on earth to be brought together in Christ (1:10); and that is being worked out now as Jew and Gentile come together as the church (1:11). It means that when the church lives as the church, the will of God is being done (5:17; 6:6). It is when we live as God's people that the purposes of God will be seen. Therefore, to understand the will of God is more than intellectual assent; it is active, day to day obedience, walking in the good works which he has prepared for us, living rightly with one another and in the world.

That is perhaps hinted at even more strongly when we think about the particular words Paul uses. In Ephesians 'Lord' language refers to Jesus. This is not simply God's will; it is the will of Jesus, the Lord and head of the church. As they 'learnt Christ' (4:17-21) so they are to walk his way.

When preaching this we may need to keep in mind that many tend to think of the Lord's will in very personal terms, relating to job or marriage or a move to a new area. And whilst God is undoubtedly sovereign over all these concerns, the real issue is how we live as God's people, whatever our marital state, the job we do or where we live.

The life of the Spirit-filled Christian (5:18-21)

The third of the three contrasts in these verses might strike us as rather unusual. We are not to 'get drunk on wine, which leads to debauchery. Instead be filled with the Spirit' (v. 18). The apparently sudden inclusion of drunkenness may not, as some suppose, relate to a particular vice in Ephesus and we should be wary of reading too much about the situation into the text. It may well have been the case that pagan worship in Ephesus involved intoxication, and that intoxication was regarded as a means of inspiration, but drunkenness is commonly cited throughout the New Testament as a characteristic of darkness. It is perhaps the most visual demonstration of the debauchery of a godless life, dulling the senses and impairing the faculties[1].

It is equally unhelpful to draw a parallel between the intoxication of the Spirit and intoxication caused by alcohol, as some have done. Although some mocked the disciples at Pentecost, many clearly saw that those they heard were praising God in language intelligible to them. Those who mocked did so out of ignorance, as a means of making sense of that which to them was unintelligible, not because the disciples were disorderly. On the contrary, a sign of the Spirit's work and presence in the life of the believer is peace and self-control (Gal. 5:22-23), neither of which could be said to be observable qualities in those who have had too much wine.

It seems that Paul has made the contrast because it is in character with the overriding distinction of the new life. Just as the new man has a new walk, so he will live in contrast to the old man whose walk is in darkness; a life

---

1   Foulkes, *Ephesians*, refers to drunkenness as 'a particular and indeed prominent manifestation of the folly of the old life' p. 155.

so often epitomised in the New Testament by drunkenness (Rom. 13:12-13; 1 Thess. 5:6-8). The 'infilling' which is required in the Christian's life issues in increasingly Christ-like qualities rather than the debauchery which comes with intoxication.

The imperative 'be filled with the Spirit' is a command to the whole Christian community and is continuous in its nature; we are to go on being filled. But it is not immediately clear what this means. The Spirit could be the agent of filling (the one who fills) or the content of filling (the one with whom we are filled), or both.

To understand this we need to allow Ephesians to shape our thinking as much as we can. We know that the church has already been described as the fullness of Jesus (1:23) and that Paul has prayed for the Ephesians to be *filled to the measure of the fullness of God* (3:19). Likewise Jesus is presented in 4:10 as the one who fills everything. We are expected to grow into that fullness (4:13) which is already ours (1:3) and we have been given the Spirit as a deposit (1:13-14). Paul has spoken of the dynamic nature of the Spirit's work in the church: God lives in us by his Spirit (2:22). Put that all together and it suggests that the work of the Spirit is such that we might grow into the fullness which is already ours and might be certain of the future to which we are heading.

The Spirit gives us that which is ours in Christ; he takes from that which belongs to Jesus and makes it known to us (John 16:14). In that sense he is the one who causes us to be filled. At the same time, there is a rich Trinitarian theme which runs throughout the letter. The church is the fullness of Christ; but God will live in us by his Spirit. What we must not do is to pull apart that which this letter holds together. The Spirit does and should fill us continually, but always so that we might grow into what we are and reach maturity in Christ. This is both active: we are to work hard at keeping the unity of the Spirit through the bond of peace (4:3), and passive: we must ourselves be continually filled by the Spirit.

The danger is that we build a theology of Spirit-filling without understanding the Ephesian purpose of these words. We must be filled by and with the Spirit in order to be the church, relating to one another in the ways explained in verses 19-21, all of which are part of this one over-arching command: 'Be filled by the Spirit ... speaking ... singing ... making music ... giving thanks ... submitting.' In other words, the characteristics of a Spirit-filled believer are being explained. These can be summarised in three basic areas:

Singing
The first three sub-commands are all about singing to one another. The three 'types' of singing may be indistinguishable (psalms, hymns and spiritual songs) but their purpose is made clear. First, we must sing to one another to instruct, edify and encourage. For this to happen, what we sing must be understood – this is not singing in tongues, for instance. But it tells us much about the purpose of our singing. Some of our singing must be 'horizontal' (to one another), for the purpose of building one another up in the Lord. Other singing must be 'vertical' as we sing and make music in our hearts to the Lord; that is, wholeheartedly sing his praises.

Such clarity of purpose in our singing may challenge much of our contemporary practice. Over the years music has shaped how people think about church and how they understand the Spirit to work in and through music. In his book *Selling Worship* Pete Ward writes, 'The observation that the theology of the church is being changed through the songs that we sing is very significant. If we add to this the realisation that the changing patterns in theology are related to the way that popular music markets and sells itself, then some important and perhaps less than positive observations can begin to be made.'[2]

Music often evokes a deeply emotional response and we must thank God both for the gift of music and the emotions we experience. But at the same time we need to be careful not to make the assumption that our emotional response is an indication of the Spirit's work. It is striking to observe what it is in music which causes an emotional reaction. Sometimes we may be deeply moved by the truths of the gospel as we praise God or sing to one another, but at other times our emotions may be generated by our cultural or musical taste, even if the words we sing are erroneous. We may find ourselves closing our eyes and raising our hands when the words are clearly written to encourage and edify those around us; or we may assume the Spirit is not present because we do not find ourselves warming to a particular music style even if the words associated with that music are profoundly Biblical. Many a church has been accused of being unspiritual by those who simply don't like particular instruments or music of a particularly style. Wonderfully, the Spirit's presence is not determined by our taste but his presence is experienced as truth is rightly obeyed and as we sing to one another for edification and to the Lord in praise.

Thanksgiving
An important sign of being a Spirit-filled believer is that we will be thankful. We have already seen this in contrast to the pagan lives of debauchery (5:4) but here the nature of

2   Pete Ward, *Selling Worship* (Bletchley: UK, Paternoster Press, 2005) p.5.

thanksgiving is expanded. It must be constant (always giving thanks), directional (to the Lord), total (for everything) and channelled (in the name of our Lord Jesus Christ). Here, then, is the recognition of what we have in Christ (as in 1:3-14) which is not dependent on circumstance, but on understanding, which is fundamental for healthy church living. It is striking how Christians who have most often complain most. Those who have little are often more grateful, realising how much they have in Christ. The Spirit-filled Christian is thankful despite his circumstances, not simply because of them.

Submission

We do not often think of submission as a result of the Spirit's work, but for those who are part of the church and are being filled by Him, mutual submission, manifest in loving service, will be an increasingly evident characteristic. It is part and parcel of what it means to love one another.

The particular word Paul uses usually refers to the relationship between an authority figure, or person of rank, and those in submission to him. Here it relates to all relationships, and is seen in patient, loving effort with one another (as in 4:2-3), expressed in different ways in different relationships (as in 5:22–6:9). Mutual submission still allows for different, godly roles within the church. Chapter 5 verse 21 needs to be considered with the rest of the ethical instruction with which it is associated.

One final point needs to be made as we look at these words. The motivation for submission is out of 'reverence' for Christ (5:21). The more accurate word 'fear' has been watered down in many translations but is a better fit. Just as the fear of the Lord is beginning of wisdom in the Old Testament (e.g. Prov. 9:10), so a right relationship with, and understanding of, Jesus is the beginning of right living. When we want to do what he wants we will begin to live rightly as the church.

From text to teaching

If this section is to be preached on its own as a free-standing unit something needs to be said about how it fits with what precedes it and what follows. Not only does it serve as Paul's conclusion to all that he has said about the right 'walk', but also it prepares us for the final ethical section which picks up on the last of the sub-commands associated with Spirit-filled living, about submitting to one another out of fear for Christ.

Introduction

It is very likely that those to whom we speak will be very familiar with some of the words in this passage but will be less aware of how and why they are here. Some will have misunderstandings about the way in which the believer is to be filled with the Spirit; others will make incorrect assumptions about how music relates to the work of the Spirit. As such, sensitivity is required, especially when our concern must be the building up of others (4:29) and the praise of God. At the same time, those very confusions can provide an effective way into the sermon. We might want to begin with a question: how do you know when someone is Spirit-filled? Or perhaps a scenario of two people in church discussing music, or the presence of the Spirit in our corporate worship. It does not require great creativity to make this very applicable and relevant from the outset.

Preaching outline – an example

A sermon could be preached with two or three points:

1. 5:15-17   Walk the right way

2. 5:18-21   The life of the Spirit-filled Christian

Or:

Be careful how you walk

1. 5:15-16   Be wise not unwise

2. 5:17   Be understanding not foolish

3. 5:18-21   Be Spirit-filled not drunk

Application

In many ways this teaching is already applied. The contrasts tell us what to do and what not to do; the sub-commands which follow the indwelling of the Spirit can be used as very real challenges in our application. If we have used the introduction to challenge some of the misunderstanding and error related to music and the Spirit, then the application at the end would be the time to ensure that correct understanding is left in the mind of the believers; our churches may have specific issues which these words address. We want to leave people wanting to 'walk' the right way, clearly understanding what it might look like to be a Spirit-filled believer.

Questions for home groups/study groups

1. 5:15 reminds us to be 'careful how we walk.' What have we already been told about our 'walk' before and after becoming a Christian?

Wisdom and folly

1. How would Paul describe wisdom and what would this look like in practice? (1:8-9; 1:17-19; 3:10)

2. How are we to make the most of every opportunity? And why? (see 5:8-14)

3. What would that mean for you personally?

Foolishness and understanding the Lord's will

1. What is the Lord's will? (1:5, 10, 11; 4:17-21; 6:6)

2. What would you expect to see, therefore, in someone who was doing the Lord's will?

3. Does this describe you? If not, where do you need to change?

Drunkenness and being filled with the Holy Spirit

1. Why do you think Paul mentions drunkenness?

2. What does it mean to be filled with the Spirit? (See 1:3, 23; 2:22; 3:19; 4:3, 13)

3. According to these verses, what would you expect to see in Spirit-filled Christians – in church, alone and in relationship with others? What is their motivation?

4. What, therefore, is the sign of a truly Spirit-filled person?

5. Does this describe you? If not, where do you need to change?

12

THE CHURCH AT HOME AND WORK (I)
(5:22-33)

It is much easier to appear authentically Christian at church than in private, at home or at work. Sometimes the only way to discover if someone is an authentic believer is by asking their spouse or children or boss. What we are when we are at work or at home is as important as what we are when we are with other believers and when we engage as a church with the world. This final section takes us to the heart of that life behind closed doors and what it means to be part of the church, God's new humanity, when the mask is off and when our church friends cannot see us. This third area of church relationships is perhaps the most challenging and controversial of all.

Before we look at the text we must also be aware that many of these words will be easily misunderstood. Particular words may trigger certain reactions and many people may be dealing with painful issues in their marriages, or particular challenges as parents or children, or in regard to their situation at work. Whilst pastoral sensitivity is never an excuse to evade the teaching of the text, we should seek to be prayerful and wise as we preach these verses.

To that end it may be sensible to deal with the section on marriage as a single sermon and then take the two subsequent 'domestic relationships' (children and parents, slaves and masters) in another sermon. However we choose to divide the passage, it is of the utmost importance that we do not cut it from its moorings, but rather see it as it is placed within this letter and therefore as part of what it means to live as God's new humanity.

Preliminary observations

All three of the relationships dealt with in 5:22 to 6:9 are examples of what submission looks like in the day to day lives of believers. 'Submitting to one another' (5:21) is a mark of the Spirit-filled Christian, defined in particular ways in the three sets of relationships which are discussed. Each has the same pattern: first the one who is subordinate is addressed, a command then follows and finally a motivation is given for that command. The word used for submission does assume a certain 'order' in which there is both someone in authority and someone in subordination, but we must be careful not to project a different, modern (or postmodern) agenda on to particular words. Any words we choose to explain this passage may be misunderstood. We would do well to heed Stott's advice:

> Even the Biblical word 'submission' is often expounded as if it were a synonym for 'subjection', 'subordination' and even 'subjugation.' All these words have emotive associations. 'Submission' is no exception. We have to try to disinfect it of these and to penetrate into its essential Biblical meaning. This we shall discover neither from its modern

associations, nor even from its etymology, but primarily from the way it is used in its context in Ephesians 5.[1]

The idea of submission certainly directs the three relationships, but always as related to what it means to be in Christ (as to the Lord, 5:22; in the Lord, 6:1; as you would obey Christ, 6:5). Right living in the domestic sphere ultimately comes from the realisation of what it means to have every spiritual blessing in Christ in the heavenly realms.

Listening to the text

(22) Wives, submit to your husbands as to the Lord. (23) For the husband is the head of the wife as Christ is the head of the church, his body, of which he is the Saviour. (24) Now as the church submits to Christ, so also wives should submit to their husbands in everything. (25) Husbands, love your wives, just as Christ loved the church and gave himself up for her (26) to make her holy, cleansing her by the washing with water through the word, (27) and to present her to himself as a radiant church, without stain or wrinkle or any other blemish, but holy and blameless. (28) In this same way, husbands ought to love their wives as their own bodies. He who loves his wife loves himself. (29) After all, no-one ever hated his own body, but he feeds and cares for it, just as Christ does the church – (30) for we are members of his body. (31) 'For this reason a man will leave his father and mother and be united to his wife, and the two will become one flesh.' (32) This is a profound mystery – but I am talking about Christ and the church. (33) However, each one of you also must love his wife as he loves himself, and the wife must respect her husband.

---

1   Stott, *Ephesians*, p. 224.

This, the longest passage in the 'household' section, provides us with the most profound and detailed description of Christian marriage in the New Testament. Although the stumbling block for many is the first verse (5:22), the instruction to husbands is more than double the length of that to their wives (115 words as compared to 40) and in many ways, far more challenging.

In the Greek text, unlike the NIV and ESV, there is no verb in 5:22. It continues from 5:21, making it clear that this is one place in which submission occurs. Submitting to one another out of fear of Christ, as a mark of Spirit-living, is now worked out in the married relationship, with instruction to wives, husbands and then to both (in the summary teaching of 5:33).

Wives (5:22-24)

Paul has spent a significant proportion of this letter reminding us what God has done in Christ to make a new humanity, which is marked by its mutual love and service and in which all previous barriers of rank and status have been abolished. We can be sure that these verses do not re-erect what the gospel has destroyed. Rather, they explain what Gospel living looks like. The fact that Paul later refers to Genesis 2:24 indicates that he has in mind the pattern given in creation rather than the perversion in relationships that resulted from the fall. Many of us will be tempted to project our non-gospel ideas and experiences on to the gospel model and therefore reject what is helpful and right by using ideas that are unhelpful and incorrect.

The form of the word used for 'submit' indicates its voluntary nature. Paul does not have coercion in mind, but rather a wilful, gospel-driven submission from wife to husband which originates from a right relationship with Jesus. It should be 'as to the Lord' (v. 22).

Having stated the nature of submission, with its imperative command, the reason for submission is given. It is because the 'husband is the head of the wife as Christ is head of the church, his body, of which he is the Saviour' (5:23). On the two occasions where the word 'head' has been used, both refer to Christ, not as the source (as some have said), but as the one who rules the church (1:22; 4:15). Fortunately, the nature of that rule has been seen. His headship is *for* the church; he has our best interests at heart. He is our saviour and from him we receive health and grow to maturity. This is the nature of headship which Paul has in view and to which wives must submit, a headship which is expressed in love and self-sacrifice (see also 5:1-2).

It is our voluntary submission to Christ which is the model for a wife's submission to her husband 'looking to its head for his beneficial rule, living by his norms, experiencing his presence and love, receiving from him gifts that will enable growth to maturity'.[2] This is not, therefore, a licence to submit to that which does not submit to Christ; rightly lived, this model can never be an excuse to promote sin. Nor is it an excuse for husbands to enforce submission. Rather, it is the kind of voluntary and joyful submission with which the believer responds to Christ.

Whilst this model of marriage is given to Christians within the church, the fact that it is rooted in creation means that it is the God-given expectation for all marriages. But without lives transformed by the gospel it can be very difficult to live up to this ideal. Most of us will be preaching into situations where there is pain, hurt and compromise within marriage. The only real solution in the pastoral

2   A.T. Lincoln, *Paradise now and not yet : Studies in the role of the heavenly dimension in Paul's thought with special reference to eschatology* (Cambridge, UK: Cambridge University Press, 1981) p. 372.

mess and muddle of most churches is the gospel which has been presented in the letter to the Ephesians. As we come to understand what it means to be in Christ, what he has done for us, then we can begin to live as we were designed to live; we can become what we are within our marriages. Paul does not address the complications of adultery or abuse in this passage, or the submission of a wife to a tyrannical non-Christian husband. He does, however, explain how we should live in the world as those who trust Christ – both in our relationship with non-Christians and how we should behave in our marriages. Other areas of scripture deal with the vexed issue of the non-Christian spouse (e.g. 1 Cor. 7:12-16). Here we must be content to see the implications for wives in submitting to their husbands within the God-given model of marriage.

Husbands (5:25-32)

The idea of submission would not have been particularly strange for Paul's first readers. What would have been more of a surprise is his command to husbands, for the way in which the husband is commanded to exercise his headship and 'rule' is through self-sacrificial love. Husbands are to love their wives 'just as Christ loved the church and gave himself up for her'. The ultimate way in which Jesus expressed his love for the church is that he died for her. The head of the church died for the church, even when those for whom he died were rebellious sinners. Our response to him was not a pre-requisite of his death but a consequence of it. There were no conditions; his actions were driven by pure undeserved grace.

The love of Christ is, of course, a model for all believers (5:1-2) and the relational expectations incumbent on all believers (as seen in chapters 4 and 5) must be seen in both parties in a marriage. At the same time, there is something unique about the relationship between husband and wife. The calling is a high one; husbands are to be concerned first and foremost with the holiness of their wives. He must have the same goal in marriage as Jesus does for his church: to sanctify her, to present her to himself and to make her holy and blameless. Each of these three goals warrants some careful consideration, both for marriages and for the church.

Sanctification brings with it the idea of being set apart for God's service. It is the practical expression of holiness, seen in the church in the ways outlined from 4:1. The start-point for this Christian service is when we come to faith in Christ, hence the close association in this verse between the declaration of holiness and the work of the Word: *to make her holy, cleansing her by the washing of water through the Word*. It was when the Ephesians heard the Word of truth that they were included in Christ (1:13). As they came under the sound of the gospel, they repented, believed and were cleansed (as in 1 Cor. 6:11). Underlying these words may well be the rich Old Testament imagery of the covenant relationship between God and his people, frequently pictured as a marriage, which in Ezekiel 16:8-14 included God's cleansing of his bride. It is helpful to have this in mind as we read these words.

That inclusion into Christ through the Word and the service that follows is not the end point for the Christian church but just the beginning. The end-point has already been explained (1:9-10). One day all things in heaven and on earth will be brought under the Lordship of Christ. When that happens Jesus will 'present to himself his glorious church' (my translation; NIV 'radiant'). Jesus not only makes the church holy by dying for us, but he will also present us to himself at the end of time.

It means that the goal of Jesus for the church, the people he loves, is that we would be rescued and perfected such that one day we will be without stain or wrinkle or any other blemish, but holy and blameless. Again, we need to remind ourselves of the wonderful hymn of praise from the beginning of the letter. God chose us in him before the creation of the world to be holy and blameless [and loving] (1:4). This is God's goal for the church, achieved through the Lord Jesus Christ. This is what Jesus wants for his people and what he is doing for his people.

The first motivation given to husbands is, therefore, a remarkably high calling. This total concern for the well-being and the future perfection of the church is the model for Christian marriage. It is both self-sacrificial (a husband should give himself up for his wife) and self-denying (a husband should put the total well-being and spiritual perfection of his wife above his own desires). This is far from the notion of headship that many will have before reading this text.

The second motivation may appear a little mundane in comparison: 'In this same way, husbands ought to love their wives as their own bodies. He who loves his wife loves himself'. (5:28) But before we crash down into narcissism, we need to think carefully about what Paul is saying. Not only does he have Genesis 2:24 in mind, where in marriage husband and wife become one flesh, but he has also just been talking about the relationship of Jesus to the church, 'which is his body, the fullness of him who fills everything in every way' (1:23; see also 4:4; 4:16). To love oneself in that context is to love the church and to love one's wife with

Christ-like perfection. The next verse amplifies and clarifies his meaning: 'After all, no-one ever hated his own body, but he feeds and cares for it, just as Christ does the church – for we are members of his body' (5:29-30).

This is a wonderfully powerful image. Not only do we care for our own bodies, feeding, washing and clothing them, but also the Lord Jesus cares for and provides for us, his church, his body. It would be unthinkable for him to do otherwise. And so it should be unthinkable for a husband to behave in any other way towards his wife. Were he to do so, he would be damaging himself in some way and distorting the picture of the gospel which marriage provides. In marriage self-care is manifest in wife-care. As husbands seek to love their wives as Christ loved the church, they will gain more self-worth and value than the rather more shallow and self-centred versions of love offered by the world.

Throughout this section Paul has had the creation mandate of Genesis 2:24 in mind, which he then quotes in 5:31. There is indeed a 'oneness' about marriage, expressed physically but also experienced at far deeper level. The first half of 5:32 might lead us to think that Paul is expressing the mystical nature of marriage, but the second half of the verse contains a surprising and astonishing twist. Paul is talking about *Christ and the church*. It is surprising because it suggests that in creation, when marriage was instituted by God, the relationship of Christ and the church was in the mind of God. It means that throughout the history of man, marriage was designed not only for the benefit of man and woman, but as a way of expressing the gospel and picturing God's end-times purposes. That is the mystery to which Paul is referring, that the relationship between Christ and the church explains marriage and that marriage is a visual aid of the gospel. This mystery has now been made known (3:5-6); astonishingly it is seen in the way in which husbands and wives relate to each other. Marriage rightly lived is a foretaste of the future (1:9-10).

Husbands and wives (5:33)

In his summary statement the roles of husband and wife are re-stated. A husband must love his wife and the wife must 'fear' her husband. This word is more often translated 'reverence' or 'respect' but suitably fits here as a mirror to the same word which appears in 5:21. Just as we should all submit to one another out of fear of Christ, so here Paul uses the same word to reflect the husband-wife relationship. He is not suggesting cowering fear but rather the quality, intimacy and dynamic of the relationship believers have with the Lord Jesus. The section began with love and submission; it ends with love and respect. As husband and wife live in this way they manifest the reality of Spirit-filled lives seen in godly headship and love, and godly submission and respect.

It is important to see the wonderful result of marriage rightly lived, both for the world (in that it proclaims the gospel) and for individuals (in that they are most likely to grow in love and holiness by living this way). Marriage has been distorted by the fall; it can be liberated by the gospel. Oppressed women will find themselves loved with a sacrificial love and oppressive men will begin to exercise biblical headship which at its core is servant-hearted love.

From text to teaching

It is perhaps because of the distorted pattern of marriage which resulted from the fall that these words can at first appear so alien to our culture. The models of marriage in the world around will often reflect an imbalance within the husband-wife relationship which is so ingrained that we do not at first realise that we view marriage through the wrong lens. There will be many who react negatively to words like 'headship' and 'submission' without allowing them to be defined by the language of Ephesians. The temptation is therefore to down-play the teaching or to over-contextualise it such that it appears no longer to apply. We need to remember that these are God's words, given to his apostle for his church. Rightly understood and rightly obeyed they will be gloriously liberating, resulting in marriages which reflect the Spirit-filled reality of the new humanity and which picture something of the end-times perfection for which we wait (1:9-10).

When preaching this section it is important to anchor it within the letter, showing how it expands the instruction to be filled with the Spirit in 5:18 and how it flows out of the mutual submission of 5:21. We will also need to remember that none of us will be 'neutral.' Rather, we will have been shaped by our fallen world and the unregenerate relationships which are all around us. Inevitably our default position is likely to be of misunderstanding what Paul is saying. We will, therefore, need to be very careful about how we introduce this passage and very clear about how we apply it.

If time allows, it may be wise and helpful to look at the ethical section of 4:1–6:9 in one unit before breaking it down into the three sections of marriage, family and work in subsequent weeks. If the material is also being used for home groups more time can be allowed for the practical application of these words, which may have profound and far-reaching implications for those under our pastoral charge.

Introduction

The preaching context may determine how we introduce a sermon on this passage. I once attended a wedding at which the preacher began by addressing the newly-married bride. In the first word of his sermon he called her by name; in his second word he simply said 'submit.' At that point those who were sitting in front of me muttered under their breaths and no longer listened. They were not believers and had no hope of understanding the gospel which lay behind Paul's instruction. It was not the wisest way in which to introduce the sermon.

Many of us will preach to mixed congregations. Some non-Christians will be present, others will be believers with less than ideal marriages; some will be struggling with singleness or the pain of divorce. A number will never have shared their difficulties in these areas.

With that in mind we need to be particularly careful and sensitive in the way we introduce this passage. This model of marriage is wonderfully liberating and edifying if rightly understood, but our first few words may determine whether or not people listen. Without seeing that this teaching comes out of what it means to be a Spirit-filled Christian (5:21), and follows teaching about the ways in which we should deal with one another in the church and the world, we may face an uphill battle. In that sense we must not make this teaching of greater significance than other teaching in this letter about what it means to be God's people and how we become what we are in Christ.

Preaching outline – an example

If 5:22-33 is preached alone, the passage naturally breaks down as follows:

1. 5:22-24   The Spirit-filled wife

2. 5:25-32   The Spirit-filled husband

    • verses 25-27   Love your wife as Christ loved
                         the church

    • verses 28-32   Love your wife as yourself

3. 5:33   The Spirit-filled marriage

Application

It would be wise to apply the passage once the verses
have been unpacked so that both husbands and wives are
addressed at the same time. It may be advantageous to
address men first in order to give some examples of what
this high calling might look like in practice. Thereafter it
becomes easier to see how wives might submit to this kind
of love and exemplify Spirit-filled living. Perhaps married
couples could be encouraged to spend some time together
thinking through the ways in which the gospel might have
more impact on their marriages – not only when seen by
others in the public arena, but in the private conversation
and behaviour which others do not see.

   If the passage is preached together with the next section,
it may be divided as follows:

Submission in action – being the church at home

1. 5:22-33   Husbands and wives
    • 5:22-24   Wives: submit, as to the Lord
    • 5:25-32   Husbands: love as the Lord loved
    • 5:33   The Spirit-filled marriage

2. 6:1-4   Parents and children

3. 6:5-9   Slaves and masters

These titles require an introduction which unpacks 5:18-21 or at least reminds those listening where this passage fits in the overall flow of the letter. Once the nature of submission is understood ('submitting to one another out of reverence to Christ', wives to your husbands, etc.), it becomes easier to unpack the three categories where this is to be worked out, thereby requiring less information in the title than might otherwise be given.

If we want to use more arresting titles (which either hint at the content or hook the listener) we need to be careful to balance the commands within the three categories. In the examples given below I have given an alternative title within the brackets, each of which seek to convey something of the imperatives within the passage:

1. 5:22-33   Marriage: submission and self-sacrifice
              (Wives submit; husbands love)

2. 6:1-4   Family life: what Dads must do
              (Children obey; fathers teach)

3. 6:5-9   Getting it right at work
              (Employees obey; employers behave)

Questions for home groups/study groups

All three relationships in 5:22–6:9 are examples of what Spirit-filled submission looks like in practice. The following questions relate specifically to the passage addressed in this chapter.

1. What difficulties might people have when they first read this passage?

2. Why do you think people might have such difficulties?

3. How does the context of Ephesians 5:22-33 help us to understand what Paul is teaching?

4. What does a Spirit-filled wife look like?

5. What is the nature of Christ's rule? (1:22; 4:15; 5:1-2)

6. What does this mean for marriage?

7. What does a Spirit-filled husband look like?

8. What should be a husband's concern for his wife? What should he do to achieve this?

9. How does Jesus love his own body? How is this reflected in marriage?

10. What was in God's mind in Genesis 2:24?

11. What does this teach us about marriage? What does it teach us about the church?

12. How do these words challenge our understanding of headship and submission? If you are married, how might you need to change as a result of these words?

13

THE CHURCH AT HOME AND WORK (II)
(6:1-9)

The previous chapter may have caused us to think carefully about how our marriages reflect God's new humanity, but as we move on in this third area of 'domestic relationships' we see what it means to be a Spirit-filled believer within the family and when out at work. The second of these areas is not directly addressed by Paul; he still has in mind the conduct of the Christian within the home. But the nature of our modern society draws us to the wider implications of this teaching as we seek to discover what it means to live as church within the world.

Preliminary observations

Paul adopts the same pattern of teaching for the two further groups he addresses in the first nine verses of chapter 6. As with the instructions to husbands and wives, the teaching must be related to 5:21 where we are asked to submit to one another out of reverence (fear) for Christ. But unlike the first section where the instruction to wives and husbands follows directly from 5:21 with no verb, here the word 'obey' governs both the relationship of children to their parents and slaves to their masters. Such 'obedience' would have been not only acceptable but also expected within the ancient world. What would have been more of a surprise is how the father and master (perhaps one and the same in the original context) should behave towards his children and his slaves in a world where he had total power, authority and rule.

Although relatively short sections, these passages can have far-reaching implications within the local church as we seek to live out the 'will of God' (5:17) during those times when we are not gathered together – in the home and when at work. For that reason I have included some initial thoughts on application after each section text.

Listening to the text

(1) Children, obey your parents in the Lord, for this is right. (2) 'Honour your father and mother' – which is the first commandment with a promise – (3) 'that it may go well with you and that you may enjoy long life on earth.' (4) Fathers, do not exasperate your children; instead bring them up in the training and instruction of the Lord. (5) Slaves, obey your earthly masters with respect and fear, and with sincerity of heart, just as you would obey Christ. (6) Obey them not only to win their favour or when their eye is on you, but like slaves of Christ, doing the will of God from your heart. (7) Serve wholeheartedly, as if you were serving the Lord, not men (8) because you know that the Lord will reward everyone for whatever good he does, whether he is slave or free. (9) And masters, treat your slaves in the same way. Do not threaten them, since you know that he who is both their Master and yours is in heaven, and there is no favouritism with him.

Children and parents (6:1-4)

This short section is a continuation of what it means to be a Spirit-filled Christian. Paul has progressed 'inwards' from our relationships in the world, to those in the church and finally to whose within the home. And now, as he continues to unpack life in the domestic sphere, he turns to the relationship between parent and child. Here then is an explanation of what 5:21 looks like in the home and how Christian children and Christian parents should relate to each other. At the heart of this relationship we find the Lord Jesus: children are to obey their parents 'in the Lord' and fathers are to bring up their children in the training and instruction 'of the Lord.'

As with all three sections, the 'subordinate' is addressed first, but unlike the relationship between husband and wife, the language is stronger. No longer is there a hint of voluntary submission; obedience is demanded and expected. In the ancient world such patterns of behaviour were the norm. Fathers had the right to behave in ways which would be deemed totally unacceptable today. They could enslave their children, force them to work and even punish by death if the crime was thought worthy of such treatment. But Paul does not rely on contemporary models of behaviour to instruct parents and children. Instead he builds his teaching on the foundation of the Bible and centres it on the Lord Jesus Christ.

Children

Children are asked to obey their parents and are then given two reasons why this command should be heeded. The first is simply that it is right, suggesting that this is God's created model for right relationships between parent and child. We should not be surprised, therefore, that in a world which has turned its back on God and is dead in sin this model will have been distorted. Paul reminds us elsewhere that disobedience of children was (and is) a sign of 'the terrible times in the last days' (2 Tim. 3:1). Conversely, obedient submission is a sign of a redeemed people, seen as the Spirit-filled child obeys his or her parents.

The second reason for obedience is rooted in the commands of the Old Testament. Paul quotes the 5th commandment (Exod. 20:12; Deut. 5:16), thereby placing the responsibility of children firmly in terms of the covenant relationship with God. Obedience to parents is part and parcel of what it means to live rightly as God's people. Yet as Paul applies this principle to the Ephesian church, two issues emerge.

The first is that he regards the 5th commandment as 'the first commandment with a promise' even though some would say that a promise has already been associated with the 2nd commandment. It could be that as there is no article in the original, Paul is regarding this commandment as of foremost significance for children; equally he may regard the wording of the 2nd commandment as referring to the character of God (punishing those who hate him and blessing those who love him) rather than the promise of God. Whatever we may conclude, it is clear that the consequence of covenant obedience for children is that 'all may go well with you and that you may enjoy a long life on the earth.'

Here the second issue comes into focus, for the wording of the 5th commandment relates to the Promised Land of the Old Testament people of God rather than simply having a good and long life on earth. Paul knows that all such promises find their fulfilment in Christ and that the new covenant equivalent of a settled and long life in the land is the rescue brought about through Christ for the future (1:9, 10, 14, 18). Whilst the fullness of the promise is yet to be experienced, the reality of God's work in Christ is seen in the local church (3:10) and the relationships of those who are a part of it. Unlike the distorted counterparts of the fallen world, the redeemed family will live out the life of blessing which has been made possible by the work of Christ which should result in all 'going well' and living a 'long life' on earth.

Before we move to the responsibility of parents, and of fathers in particular, we may need to consider the scope of this command. Children who have reached maturity in the eyes of the law may not be thinking of obeying their parents in the same way as those who are still under the care and provision of the parental home. All of us, whatever age we are, have a responsibility to honour our parents, but there is clearly no sense of adult command to adult. Equally, although this command is given to the church, and therefore presumes mutual Christian understanding, there will need to be pastoral consideration as to how believing children in an unbelieving home should behave. Allegiance to Christ will mean that children should be obedient to their parents, but surely not in cases where children may be forced to renounce their faith or behave in knowingly ungodly ways.

Fathers

Fathers are addressed specifically, even though children must obey their *parents*. This may reflect both the biblical and cultural responsibility the fathers had as heads of households and does not mean that mothers can abdicate the responsibilities outlined here. But in our culture, where so often men abdicate spiritual and practical responsibility for bringing up children, this command is particularly apposite. Fathers must take responsibility for their children.

Negatively, fathers should not 'exasperate' their children. The word used suggests the idea of not being provoked to wrath. John Stott helpfully highlights how this might happen: 'Parents can easily misuse their authority either by making irritating or unreasonable demands which make no allowances for the inexperience or immaturity of children, or by harshness and cruelty at one extreme or by favouritism and over-indulgence at the other, or by humiliating or suppressing them, or by those two vindictive weapons of sarcasm or ridicule.'[1] Clearly all these damaging traits can result from misuse of the position of authority of the father.

Positively, fathers are asked to bring children up in the 'training and instruction of the Lord.' This concept of nurture makes use of the same word as in 5:29, relating both to how we look after ourselves and how the Lord nourishes the church in his work of bringing us to holiness and perfection. The way in which a father is to do this is by 'training and instruction.' The first of these words can be used of training or education in general or discipline and chastisement in particular. It is the word Paul chooses to use when explaining the role of the Old Testament, 'training in righteousness' (2 Tim. 3:16) which suggests that he understands it as something which shapes those to whom it is applied. The second word ('instruction' [NIV, ESV] 'admonition' [RSV]) is also used elsewhere to explain the purpose of the scriptures (1 Cor. 10:11) and in that context has a more corrective role.

Together it is clear that Paul has the total spiritual and moral well-being of the child in view, behind which not only stands the Lord (it is 'his' instruction) but which also has

---

1   Stott, *Ephesians*, p. 246.

the Lord as its object. What Paul desires for all people who are in Christ so also he desires for children, nurtured within the family by their fathers in such a way that children grow up to know, love and obey the Lord Jesus.

Application

The vast majority of children who hear these words preached within our churches will come from Christian households and therefore it is important that the sermon addresses them in particular. That may beg the question as to how that might be best achieved given our models of Sunday school and the inevitable lack of children who sit under the Word within the gathered congregation.

The fact that children were addressed by Paul presumes that they were a part of the gathering and not separated from their parents into age-appropriate teaching classes. This should not necessarily lead us to jettison our inherited models of Sunday school, but it might give us cause to question how we might achieve the mutual teaching of parent and child where both 'hear' what each other should be doing and how the instruction relates to the rest of the letter. Perhaps it would be wise at this point in a sermon series not to have the usual Sunday school gathering but to address both young and old in the main meeting. Alternatively, the Sunday school teaching series could run parallel with the main sermon series with practical worked-out examples for 'homework' for parents with their children. However we choose to tackle this teaching, both its content and its inclusion as teaching to the whole church might challenge us to think through what we do, why we do it and how we do it. Ephesians reminds us how the gospel creates a new community; we must be careful not to engage in a practice which might divide it.

There is also a challenge as to how we might best teach children within the home. Many families rely on mothers taking the initiative to teach and train the children, with relatively little spiritual input from their fathers. Those of us who are men need to think through how this can be done in the midst of other daily pressures and the constantly changing needs of growing children.

Slaves and masters (6:5-9)

The fact that Paul does not make any social comment about slavery should not cause us to conclude that its practice was, or is, acceptable. In 1 Timothy 1:10 Paul condemns slave trading (the 'stealing' of men for profit) as that which opposes the gospel and sound teaching, but even with such a prohibition, the presence of slaves in the ancient world was not universally negative. The Roman Empire relied on their work, not only as labourers and servants, but also as teachers, doctors and administrators. Some slaves were treated very badly, but others were treated with care as valued and valuable 'property.'

What should surprise us is that both slaves and masters are addressed together, as members of one church. It is clear that those who had come to Christ in Ephesus have already realised the counter-cultural reality of this new community, where our relationship to Christ rather that our position in society determines our identity. Both slave and master must have gathered together as they listened to the teaching of Paul.

As with the previous two sections, the 'subordinate' is addressed first.

Slaves

Slaves must obey their earthly 'lords' with *fear and trembling*. This couplet is usually reserved for our standing before God and may well have been included to remind the slaves

that they work as *if serving the Lord* (6:7). But it also takes
us back to 5:21, from which all this teaching is derived. Just
as we should submit to one another out of reverence (fear)
for Christ, so also in the same way slaves should obey their
earthly masters with respect (fear) and trembling. It is the
Lord Jesus Christ who lies behind the instruction; whatever
is done must be done as if to him.

The two characteristics of this service are that it must
be consistent (even when the master is not looking)
and it must be wholehearted, as a slave not simply of an
earthly master but as a slave of Christ, a position held by
all authentic Christians. Even though many slaves of the
ancient world may have worked only out of fear of their
masters, Christians should be different.

The motivation for this command once again takes us
to the end times (6:8 cf. 1:9-10). Whether we are slave or
free, well treated or badly treated, the reality is the same for
everyone: God will reward us for what we do. Here again
we face the biblical tension between God's responsibility
and ours. We are created in Christ Jesus for a new walk,
with good works prepared for us in advance by God (2:10).
But that new work and the works related to it are seen as we
make an effort and seek to be obedient to the Word as it is
taught; that is the will of God. And a Spirit-filled Christian
understands the will of the Lord (5:17), not only in the
sense of what God has done for us in Christ (1:5, 9, 11) but
how that will is worked out in the lives of his people.

Masters
The instruction to masters would have been very shocking
to the ancient world. Seneca quotes a Roman saying that
'all slaves are enemies'[2]. Yet here Paul tells masters that they

---

2   Seneca, *Epistlae Morales*, 47.5.

should treat their slaves in the same way (6:9); in other words, in the same way in which they might expect their slaves to respect and 'fear' them. The practical outworking of this instruction sets Christian masters up in distinction to their unbelieving counterparts who could behave as they wished. The Christian master must not threaten his slaves (thereby not relying on fear of the master for results), but rather treat them with respect, as those who are brothers in Christ (with 'fear' rightly directed towards him). Their actions should be controlled and governed by the knowledge that they themselves have a higher master to whom, one day, they will be answerable. Slave and master, therefore, stand before their heavenly master in exactly the same way. The world's status or position, by birth or effort, means nothing in the church of God. Christ's Lordship affects all earthly relationships.

Application

Slavery is still a problem in the world yet the total number of slaves in the world is thought to be the lowest recorded number in history (figures vary from 12 to 27 million). It is thus unlikely that those to whom we preach will be caught in slavery (although sensitivity to debt problems and human trafficking must not be overlooked).

Even though these words may have initially been applied to the relationships within Ephesian families, there is a legitimate link between the first century role of slaves and our modern working relationships. Both employer and employee have responsibilities to behave in right ways if they belong to Christ. Indeed, our behaviour in the working environment, our attitude to those who work with us or for us, or those for whom we work, is part and parcel of what it means to be the church. The reality of Spirit-filled submission to the Lord Jesus should be seen in the way we relate to those we meet in our working environment. The new humanity and the picture of the future which it presents pervades all areas of our lives.

From text to teaching

Although it is possible to preach the third 'ethical' section in one sermon (5:22–6:9) it will inevitably mean that we are forced to leave out some of the detail or to give less time to application. This teaching could be broken into two sermons, by taking 5:22-33 as one unit and 6:1-9 as the other, or into three, by taking each relationship one at a time (wives-husbands, children-parents and slaves-masters), which would be the preferred option if time allows.

To a certain extent our context will determine what is the best course of action. It may be that if we are combining a sermon series with home group material, the application can be worked through more carefully in a small group setting. Whatever we decide it is important that each part must be related both to 5:21 and to the overall shape of the letter.

Introduction

An introduction to 6:1-9 needs to challenge the hearers about their contemporary practice, perhaps by asking how you can spot a Spirit-filled father or employee. A gentle question to fathers could be very instructive, such as, 'if I were to ask your children what you have taught them about the Christian faith, what would they say?' Or a question to those who work, 'what is it about how you do what you do that indicates you are part of God's new humanity?'

If we have children present we need to think more carefully about how we introduce this material, not only because it addresses them specifically but also because of the opportunity it presents for parents and children to sit together under the Word and listen to teaching directly impacting their relationship. If this is to be the case we would be wise to consider taking the three relationships as three separate sermons.

Preaching Outlines – examples

1. 6:1-4   The church at home – how to be Christian when no-one sees

    • 6:1-3   Children: obey your parents

    • 6:4   Fathers: don't make them angry; teach them

2. 6:5-9   The church at work – how to be a Christian for all to see

    • 6:5-8   Employees: work as if working for Jesus

    • 6:9   Employers: serve with your master in mind

Or, alternatively:

1. 6:1-4   The Christian at home

    • 6:1-3   The Christian child – obey don't rebel

    • 6:4   The Christian parent – educate don't exasperate

2. 6:5-9   The Christian at work

    • 6:5-8   Obey your boss – as you would Jesus

    • 6:9   Serve your workers – as you would Jesus

Application

In addition to the general points already made, it is worth considering specific examples of how this teaching might look in practice. How do parents in general and fathers in particular bring their children up in the training and instruction of the Lord? Undoubtedly this will involve suggestion and guidance about teaching the Bible in the home but thought will also need to be given to the home environment, the rules and privileges allowed and how children can best be nurtured and nourished as Christians.

Likewise, consideration will need to be given to the nature of the working environment and issues of godliness which might arise from Christian living with a boss who does not share the same ethical values. In raising such questions it must be noted that Paul is not dealing with the situation experienced by those to whom Peter was writing (1 Pet. 2:18-24), some of whom were being treated badly, but rather those who have already acknowledged Jesus as Lord and Saviour and need to know how to live out their faith in the domestic sphere.

It is likely that there will be pastoral implications resulting from preaching these passages, some of which are unforeseen, for which time may need to be set aside – both personally in pastoral counselling and perhaps also within home groups or a church prayer meeting.

Questions for home groups/study groups

Parents and children

1. How should children behave and why? (See also 2 Tim. 3:2)

2. Who should teach the children?

3. How should fathers behave in the home?

4. How does this challenge our contemporary models of church and our parenting?

Slaves and masters

No comment is made here about slavery (but see 1 Tim. 1:10). Paul is addressing the very real concerns with the Ephesian church – but note that slaves and masters can be addressed together, suggesting that they were not segregated in the church. The modern equivalent would probably be the work place.

1. If you are employed, how should you behave at work and why?

2. If you are an employer, how should you behave at work and why?

Summary Questions

1. What does a Spirit-filled believer look like at work and at home?

2. How does this relate to the rest of Ephesians?

3. Where do you need to change?

14
WHY CHURCH IS SO HARD (6:10-20)

Many of us are very familiar with the words of Ephesians 6:10-20. They provide wonderful imagery for family services as we talk about Roman soldiers with the aid of a willing member of the Sunday school, suitably clad in recently-constructed armour. But we need to be careful, for although these words are rightly used to explain spiritual warfare, their connection with the rest of the letter is often forgotten. The consequence of such free-floating theology is either a dualism (in which we are unsure as to whether Satan or Jesus will eventually win) or a distorted view of the devil (in which he is either given too much power or too little).

We must allow the language and concerns of Paul's letter to shape our understanding of the battle in which we are engaged, how it is manifest and how it is fought. As we do so, we will begin to realise that these words are intimately connected to what we have already discovered and explain why it is often so difficult to live as the people we have been made to be. These verses explain the spiritual reality behind 'becoming what you are.'

Preliminary observations

The rich metaphor which runs through these verses may have had its origins in the armour of a Roman soldier, but we must not assume that Paul decided upon such imagery because of his imprisonment. That may or may not be true; we simply do not know. We do, however, know that much of this imagery finds its origin in the Old Testament, that treasury of truth which the great apostle would have had at his fingertips, and that all of it relates to the theology and practice which Paul has written about in the preceding chapters. Many of the words and ideas employed have already been expressed and explained. It means that much of our work in preparing this passage will involve seeing how Ephesians shapes our understanding of power, Satan, the heavenly realms, truth, righteousness, peace, faith etc. Only then will we have the confidence that we are handling the passage with the concepts in the apostle's mind rather than in our own.

The passage naturally falls into three sections, in which the Ephesians are asked to Be Strong (6:10-12), Stand Firm (6:13-17) and Pray (6:18-20).

Listening to the text

(10) Finally, be strong in the Lord and in his mighty power. (11) Put on the full armour of God so that you can take your stand against the devil's schemes. (12) For our struggle is not against flesh and blood, but against the rulers, against the authorities, against the powers of this dark world and against the spiritual forces of evil in the heavenly realms. (13) Therefore put on the full armour

of God, so that when the day of evil comes, you may be able to stand your ground, and after you have done everything, to stand. (14) Stand firm, then, with the belt of truth buckled around your waist, with the breastplate of righteousness in place, (15) and with your feet fitted with the readiness that comes from the gospel of peace. (16) In addition to all this, take up the shield of faith, with which you can extinguish all the flaming arrows of the evil one. (17) Take the helmet of salvation and the sword of the Spirit, which is the word of God. (18) And pray in the Spirit on all occasions with all kinds of prayers and requests. With this in mind, be alert and always keep on praying for all the saints. (19) Pray also for me, that whenever I open my mouth, words may be given me so that I will fearlessly make known the mystery of the gospel, (20) for which I am an ambassador in chains. Pray that I may declare it fearlessly, as I should.

Be strong (6:10-12)

As Paul draws to a conclusion he encourages his readers to be 'empowered in the Lord and in the might of his strength.' Such 'power' has already been revealed in the resurrection and ascension of Jesus Christ (1:19-20) as God took him from the grave and placed him at his right hand, in the heavenly realms, far above all rule and authority. And that power is now also 'at work' in us as God's rescued people (3:16, 20). So when Paul writes of the power and might of God at the end of his letter we are not left in the dark as to what he means. The power and might which makes us strong is that which has been demonstrated in the resurrection and is already at work within those who believe.

The way in which we are to be made strong in that power is to put on the full armour of God and the reason we need to do that is so that we can take our stand against the devil's schemes. If we are to 'walk' the right way (picking up the language of Ephesians) we need to be aware that we do so in the face of Satan. He seeks to undermine that which God seeks to create. Here we get to the heart of all the problems that lie behind the difficulties we often experience in being church. Satan has been mentioned twice already in the letter, first as the one under whose authority we once lived (2:2) and secondly as the one who is able to get a foothold in our church relationships (4:27). He does not want us to become part of the people of God, and once we have responded to Jesus, he does not want us to live like the people of God.

It should not surprise us, therefore, that evangelism is so difficult. It requires the resurrection power of God to change our status from being objects of wrath, under the authority of Satan, to being children of God, spiritually raised with Christ. That power is manifest in the gospel: we were included in Christ (and therefore spiritually raised with him) when we heard the Word of truth (1:13). Equally, it should not surprise us that living as church is so difficult. Once we have become part of God's people, with a radically new set of relationships, marked by love and service and unity, it will be those very relationships which Satan seeks to destroy, which is why we give him a foothold when we live in any way which is inconsistent with being a part of God's new humanity (4:27). When we rightly live as God's new creation, the principalities and powers in the heavenly realms look at the church and see the wisdom of God in operation (3:10). It is as if Satan, defeated by the blood of Jesus on the cross, looks at the church and in seeing a picture of the future, realises that his days are numbered. The church reminds the devil that his destruction is near.

When the church lives as the church, Satan sniffs the smoke of the lake of fire (Rev. 20).

Ephesians might also help us to realise why it is always a battle to keep the Bible as the foundation of the church (2:20). It is the Word, rightly taught and obeyed, which will bring about that which God has created in Christ. Chapter 4 has reminded us that we become what we are by obeying the Word in acts of ministry one to another. As we do that, so we grow up in maturity, love, unity and service; we become the people we have been made to be. Take the Bible away, or distort it, and we are left as children in the faith, mere infants, blown around by every wind of teaching and marked not by patience, love, humility and gentleness, but impatience, a lack of love, pride and arrogance.

All our difficulties in being church, in becoming what we are, stem from the schemes of Satan. 'Our struggle is not against flesh and blood but against the rulers, against the authorities, against the powers of this dark world and against the spiritual forces of evil in the heavenly realms' (6:12).

Many commentators devote time to discussing the various suggestions as to what this list of evil might refer, but it seems more in keeping with Ephesians to see everything that seeks to undermine the church as ultimately coming from the evil one. He does not want us to be what we have been made in Christ. Our battle is spiritual; and it is fought in the heavenly realms even though it is manifest very firmly in our earthly experience.

At this point we could so easily miss the significance of what Paul is saying. He began his letter by reminding us that we already have every spiritual blessing in Christ in the heavenly realms (1:3). We have been raised and seated with him (2:6). But the place Jesus occupies in the unseen heavenly realms has also been explained for us. God raised him from the dead and 'seated him at his right hand in the heavenly realms, far above all rule and authority, power and dominion, and every title that can be given, not only in the present age but also in the one to come. And God placed all things under his feet and appointed him to be head over everything for the church' (1:20-22).

The place from which the Lord Jesus rules the church and the world is *above* the realm from which Satan throws his fiery darts. Our battle may be against the authorities in the heavenly realms but the Lord Jesus is in that place of total authority over him. And wonderfully, miraculously, we are there too, for spiritually we have been raised with Christ and seated with him in the heavenly realms. It is as we understand who we are in Christ (explained for us in 1:3-14) that we can begin to fight this fight and to live as God's people, for we too, in Christ, find ourselves spiritually *above* Satan's authority. That is why we have to put on *his* armour, 'the armour of God' and, as we shall see from the Old Testament, the armour of his Messiah in battle. Jesus has been placed above all rule and authority *for the church* (1:22) and it is when we live as those who are in Christ that we can indeed be the church as God intended.

Stand firm (6:13-17)

We know all too well that we live in evil days (5:16) but here Paul focuses the difficulties on one particular day of evil (6:13). It may refer to a time of particular trial and pressure which the Ephesians would one day face, or it may be understood more generally as that which can face any generation of Christians at any time. Whatever the extent of the persecution and hostility Christians experience, we need to be aware of the constant spiritual battle which seeks to undermine our Christian walk and our witness as church.

Two verbs are used and two main lists of armour from the Old Testament are employed. The two verbs (withstand/resist and stand) suggest both being able to face the onslaught and also standing one's ground as it happens. The two lists are in Isaiah 11:4-5 and Isaiah 59:17.

Isaiah 11:4-5

> But with righteousness he will judge the needy, with justice he will give decisions for the poor of the earth. He will strike the earth with the rod of his mouth; with the breath of his lips he will slay the wicked. Righteousness will be his belt and faithfulness the sash around his waist.

Isaiah 59:17a

> He put on righteousness as his breastplate and the helmet of salvation on his head.

As we search through the pages of this letter we will discover that each piece of armour relates both to that which is revealed in the gospel and also that which becomes ours in the Lord Jesus Christ; the objective reality of that which we are given and the subjective experience of the Christian as we receive it and are obedient to it.

The belt of truth (6:14)

Truth holds all things together. We were included in Christ and became part of the church when we heard the Word of truth (1:13). As a result we are to speak 'truth in love' (4:15) and live according to the truth that is in Jesus (4:21). Living 'truthfully' and speaking truthfully (4:25) are marks of being children of light (5:8). Those who are in Christ know the truth, can speak the truth and demonstrate the truth in their relationships with one another and in contrast with the world.

Satan, on the other hand, is the 'father of lies' (John 8:44) who stands in direct contrast to the truth and righteousness embodied in the Messiah. He not only distorts the objective truth of God's Word (Gen. 3:1; Luke 4:9-10) but seeks to distort the truthfulness of those who have responded to that Word (Matt. 5:37; Eph. 4:27). The only way in which we can stand against his crafty schemes is to flee to the one who is truth and whose greater power is already at work within us (3:20).

The breastplate of righteousness (6:14)

As a breastplate, righteousness covers us. In that sense it is legitimate to think of righteousness as that which has been imputed; we were made alive even when we were dead, we were made children even when we were enemies, we were raised with Christ when we deserved God's wrath. But also it is the outworking of having been made righteous. We are now able to be 'like God' in our behaviour, concerned with righteousness and holiness (4:24; 5:9).

Both these areas will be attacked by Satan. Those who know something of the contemporary church debate will be aware of how the doctrines related to imputed righteousness and the nature of justification still rouse controversy. All of us will be conscious of how difficult it can be to live out the ethical standards of righteousness as expected by the apostle (e.g. 4:24; 5:9).

In the midst of such battles Ephesians reminds us that we are only what we are because of Christ and that we can only be what we are when we are empowered by Christ. To that end we once again flee to him; it is his breastplate

of righteousness with which we are to fight the battle
(Isa. 59:17).

*Feet fitted with the readiness that comes from the gospel of peace
(6:15)*
This is a slightly unusual expression which can be difficult
to understand. Rather than mentioning a particular type of
footwear, Paul writes about its purpose and effect ('shoeing
the feet with the readiness of the gospel'). Not only do
we have the difficulty of understanding what these words
mean, but as an item of clothing the shoes are not directly
derived from the Old Testament passages already cited.
As the word 'readiness' appears nowhere else in the New
Testament it can be difficult to know exactly what it means.
In other contemporary writings it refers to preparedness
or steadfastness, both of which have a slightly different
meaning, but may equally help us understand the metaphor
employed. It is probable that Paul had another image from
Isaiah in his mind when he wrote these words:

> How beautiful on the mountains are the feet of those who
> bring good news, who proclaim peace, who bring good
> tidings, who proclaim salvation. (Isa. 52:7)

The messenger who proclaimed these words was bringing
a message of peace and reconciliation and a reminder that
God reigns. Likewise the message of the gospel brings
peace, both with God (2:1-10) and with one another (2:11-
22). In that sense, we are made ready by the gospel of peace,
that is, we are made into the people God wants us to be,
a people who demonstrate both the reality of God's wisdom
and the future demise of Satan. The effect of the gospel on
our lives is that we become a new humanity where peace
has replaced conflict, where barriers have been removed and

in which all are united together in their relationship with God because of the blood of Jesus Christ. Peace is a mark of the new community (4:3).

But the gospel of peace also radiates from that community as we live in the world (5:8-16). Just as we were included in Christ when we heard the word of truth, so also it is possible for others to be included as they hear that same word from us and see the effect of the gospel in our lives. In that sense these 'gospel shoes' not only represent what we have become in Christ but also the message of Christ which we can now share with the world: a message of peace with God and with one another through the Lord Jesus Christ.

Both aspects of this gospel reality will be attacked by Satan. He does not want us to live as God's people and he does not want the gospel to be proclaimed. As Christians engaged in a battle to be church and in a battle to win people for Christ we need to be aware that our peace as church (with one another and with God) and the gospel we proclaim will be attacked. We will discover that we need not only to teach the truth of this letter to overcome him, but we will also need the prayers of this letter which remind us of the power which is at work within us to overcome Satan and to manifest this peace.

The shield of faith (6:16)
The shield of faith has a particular function. It is to extinguish all the flaming arrows of the evil one. Martyn Lloyd-Jones classified these arrows in terms of thoughts, imaginations, desires, passions, lusts, temptations and the fiery trials of 1 Peter 1:6.[1] But the image may apply

---

1   D.M. Lloyd-Jones, *The Christian Soldier: An Exposition of Ephesians 6:10-20* (Edinburgh, UK: The Banner of Truth Trust, 1997) pp. 300-3.

equally to anything which seeks to undermine our identity in Christ. We will all face a barrage of attacks on our holiness, our prayer life, our Bible reading, our relationship with other Christians and our proclamation of the gospel in the world. Such is the work of Satan and his fiery arrows.

Faith is the shield with which we not only resist but also extinguish these arrows. Their intended effect is immediately rendered powerless by faith, which, in terms of Ephesians, is a gift given by God which unites us with Christ (2:8). It enables us to approach God freely with the confidence not only that we are in him and with him but also that he is in us (3:17). We grow in that faith, becoming what we are, as we obey the Word by serving one another in acts of ministry (4:13). Faith is not trying to convince ourselves of things for which we have no evidence, but the confidence and trust in Christ which unites us with him. And it is when we are confident and certain about who we are in Christ, raised with him and enjoying every spiritual blessing in the heavenly realms (1:3; 2:6), that we are able to stand against the devil's schemes. His fiery arrows may seek to undermine what God has created in Christ; he may attempt to prevent us living as we were meant to live, but he is overcome as we understand with greater clarity what we have and are in Christ.

The helmet of salvation (6:17)
This comes directly from Isaiah 59 and refers to the helmet which the Lord wore in victory as he saved his people and judged their enemies. Having achieved salvation himself ('his own arm worked salvation for him and his own righteousness sustained him', Isaiah 59:16), the helmet

signifies what he has done and what he can do.[2] In using the metaphor of a helmet we need not assume that it is the protection of our head (and therefore our mind) which is under attack. Although Satan may distort truth and thereby erroneously challenge our thinking, the picture here is far more about what has already been achieved by Jesus. He has secured the victory by his death and resurrection (as in 2:4-8 etc). Now, by God's grace we stand in that victory. Our salvation is secure.

The fact that there needs to be a conscious donning of this helmet means that Satan will attack our assurance of salvation or our belief in the efficacy of the cross. The helmet reminds us that Jesus has done all that is necessary; we are eternally secure. He has done everything for us to be right with God, raised with Christ and made a part of the new humanity of God's people. Through God's grace and mercy that helmet has been made ours.

The sword of the Spirit, the Word of God (6:17)
The sword is the only offensive weapon in the list of armour. There is probably little significance in the fact that Paul uses the word 'rhema' rather than 'logos' to describe the Word of God. What is of more importance is that fact that the Spirit makes the sword powerful and effective. Isaiah 11:4 reminds us that 'He will strike the earth with the rod of his mouth' – his Word - and Paul's lengthy explanation of the centrality of the Word taught and obeyed in Ephesians 4 shows us how that happens. When people first come to faith it is because they heard the Word of truth (1:13); it

2   'When the Lord dons this clothing he is publicly revealing what he is. But he is also declaring what he intends to do and that he is able to do it. It is a work which will display and satisfy his righteousness, save his people, repay his foes and be carried to completion by the driving motivation of his zeal.' Alec Motyer, *The Prophecy of Isaiah* (Nottingham, UK: IVP, 1993) p. 491.

is powerful enough to rescue people from death and wrath and to raise them with Christ, so that now they have access to the Father by one Spirit, and by that same Spirit have a guaranteed future. The Word is also needed for the church to become the church. The way in which we become the people God has made us to be (the dwelling in which God lives by his Spirit 2:22) is by the Word taught and obeyed. The Word will enable us to become mature, unified and loving; the Word obeyed enables the spiritual reality of what we are in Christ to grow and develop.

At each point in the life and growth of the church then, the Word, as the sword of the Spirit, is active. The Word is God's instrument to bring us into the family of the church, in which he dwells by his Spirit. And we are to maintain the unity of the Spirit by obedience to the Word. The spiritual reality of church becomes evident as the Word is central and is obeyed. Only then will the works of Satan be foiled; only then will we not only prevent attack, but grow stronger in the face of it.

Pray (6:18-20)

Although not part of the metaphorical armour, prayer is the other offensive weapon which works alongside the Word of God – and as such Paul spends more time writing about prayer than the other weapons in the list. Prayer clearly needs to pervade every aspect of our spiritual battle. We should engage in *all* kinds of prayer on *all* occasions for *all* the saints and should do so with *all* perseverance (NIV 'keep on praying').

'Praying in the Spirit' links us in with the concerns of the letter. The Spirit guarantees the future for which we have been saved (1:9-10). The new humanity now has access to God by one Spirit (2:18); we are being built together to become a dwelling in which God lives by his Spirit (2:22). God has revealed the gospel by the Spirit to his holy apostles and prophets (3:5) and because of what God has done for us in Christ, Paul prays that we might be strengthened with power through the Spirit (3:16) in order that Christ may be central to everything.

Both of Paul's earlier prayers (1:15-23 and 3:14-20), which provide a wonderful example of how we should pray, recognise the work of the Spirit in bringing to fruition the reality of the new humanity. And just as Paul has *not stopped* (1:16) in his prayers, so we also should pray 'on all occasions with all kinds of prayers and requests ... for all the saints' (6:18).

The emphasis here is not so much on the variety of content but the variety of prayer we can adopt in order to request the given will of God to be done. The Christian should be 'praying at all times in the Spirit with all prayer and supplication' (ESV). It is, more literally 'by means of all prayer and petition, praying at every time in the Spirit, and to it, watching in all perseverance and praying concerning the saints.' Paul has made it very clear what God wants and prayer is the way in which we ask God to do it. Truly spiritual prayer will be far more concerned with the proclamation of the gospel and the growth of the church than it will be about the concerns which dominate many of our church prayer meetings. Indeed, in our weakness we may say with Paul that 'we do not know what we ought to pray for' (or perhaps better 'how we ought to pray') and we may acknowledge that 'the Spirit himself intercedes for us with groans that words cannot express', but that work of the Spirit in interceding for us is always 'in accordance with God's will' (Rom. 8:26, 27), a will which has clearly been revealed to the Ephesians.

So the Ephesians should pray for the saints, that is, for one another. They should also pray for Paul with two particular requests in mind. They are to ask God that he will be given the words to say and that he will make them known boldly or fearlessly (the word is repeated in v. 19 and v. 20). His request is, therefore, for clarity and courage. He wants to have the right words to explain this gospel and he wants to do it boldly and without fear. Despite being in prison he does not ask the Ephesians to pray for his release, his health or his personal needs. He simply asks that this life-giving and life-changing gospel would go out from him clearly, faithfully and fearlessly.

In these last three verses Paul has exposed his real concerns: that the non-Christians may hear the gospel and that the Christians may grow rightly as part of the church, knowing who they are in Christ. The proclamation of Christ and growing into what we are in Christ: may our churches be full of such prayer.

From text to teaching

There are many potential dangers in preaching this passage, not least because many will think they know it already. It is very important to keep it rooted in the letter and to understand the terms used as Paul employs them. There is great temptation to explain what Roman armour looked like and then to create a theology from our imagery. Whilst we must concede that Paul might have wanted us to think in those ways, we are on much safer territory if we let the letter, and the Old Testament, shape our understanding. This is all about what we are in Christ and the need to live that out in the spiritual battle in which we are engaged.

But a battle it is. The unloving conversations over coffee after church, the small but very real relational tension in church, the barriers between young and old, newcomers and old-timers, locals and incomers, are all manifestations of this spiritual battle. Where Christianity is not lived out in the home or workplace, where it isn't properly taught, where the world is influencing the church: all are points at which Satan can attack. We need to be very aware of the reality of this battle and the way in which we are instructed to deal with it.

Lastly, but by no means least, this passage should shape the content of our prayers and encourage people to pray. We would do well not only to encourage more people to attend the church prayer meeting as a result of these words, but also to give more time at the end of the sermon to prayer – real, biblical, Ephesian, church-building prayer.

Introduction

This passage provides a wonderful finale to the great themes of Ephesians and reminds us that 'being church' can only be achieved in the heat of spiritual battle. Paul's choice of imagery and use of words is deeply rooted in, and connected to, all that has gone before and reaches right to the heart of the practical day to day lives of Christians. The armour reminds us that we are dependent on the Lord Jesus for everything and that we have two 'attacking' weapons at our disposal – the Word and prayer.

This passage, perhaps more than any other, connects to the very real experience of church life – the challenges to keep reading our Bible and to pray, the battles we face in our own walk with the Lord as well as our Christian service and our relationship with our fellow believers. It is both reassuring and challenging to understand why life as a believer is as it is, but also encouraging to know that there is a God-given means of overcoming Satan and that the 'walk' of the new humanity is possible.

Preaching outline – an example
The outline is simple, but it picks up Paul's concerns:

1. 6:10-12   Be Strong   – there is a battle

2. 6:13-17   Stand Firm   – there is a way

3. 6:18-20   Pray   – there is a need

Application
The application of this passage is very real: in terms of our understanding of the battle, of the need to stand firm, of the nature of the armour and of what we are in Christ. But there are two direct applications that arise from the two 'offensive' weapons, which are a challenge to all Christians and essential for the health of all churches: the place of the Bible and the place of prayer in our local congregations.

However, we must be aware of the danger of generalisations. Too many sermons end with the exhortation to read the Bible and pray more as if those activities are an end in themselves. Paul's concern for the Ephesians is not simply that they might know more and pray more but that in knowing and praying they might be able to 'stand' which, ironically, means to 'walk' the walk of the new humanity. His desire in prayer is both for the health of the church and the growth of the church and in that sense there is something more tangible about the application of his words. Rightly obeyed, they should lead to greater personal holiness and more authentic relationships within the church. They should help us to understand why it is often so difficult to achieve the picture of church presented in this letter and what it is we might do when those points of attack or discouragement come. Most importantly, we will increasingly be those who are determined to 'live a life worthy of the calling we have received' (4:1), in church, in the world and at home. As we do that, God's wisdom will be manifest to the rulers and authorities in the heavenly realms (3:10). To him be the glory in the church and in Christ Jesus throughout all generations, for ever and ever. Amen.

Questions for home groups/study groups

1. What has Paul already told us about power?

2. Read Isaiah 11:4-5; 52:7; 59:17 and make a list of all the armour mentioned in these verses. To whom does it belong and how is it employed?

3. According to Ephesians, what are the devil's schemes? (2:2; 4:27). What does he not want to see in the church?

4. What do we already know about the heavenly realms? (1:3; 1:20-23; 2:6; 3:10). What does that tell us about our place in relation to Satan?

5. Look through each piece of armour and see how it relates to the rest of the letter. What are we told about truth, righteousness, the gospel, peace and faith?

6. How do we 'obtain' all these pieces of armour? (Note 1:3)

7. What, then, do we have to do to withstand the onslaught of Satan and to stand on the day of evil?

8. What does the Word do? (1:13; 4:11-13)

9. How does the work of the Word relate to the work of the Spirit? (1:13; 2:17, 18, 22; 4:3).

10. What would happen if the Word were not central to the church, or not obeyed?

11. What does it mean to pray in the Spirit?

12. How should we pray and for whom should we pray? (Note the content of Paul's prayers 1:15-23; 3:14-19.)

13. What does Paul ask for?

14. How do these prayers compare with ours? Where do you need to change?

15

FAREWELL EPHESIANS (6:21-24)

We may decide not to preach a final sermon on these last few verses, but they warrant at least some study, for as Paul signs off and hands his missive to Tychicus for delivery, something of his heart and concern for the Ephesians is revealed afresh and the personal nature of his ministry and the believers' response to Jesus becomes clear.

Preliminary observations

The final four verses of the letter fall into two distinct sections. The first section (vv. 21-22) explains the role of Tychicus in relation to the Ephesians; the second (vv. 23-24) adopts a fairly common pattern of ancient letter-writing but Christianises it, ensuring that the Ephesians are left with the great themes of the letter: grace and peace, experienced by those who have come to know and love the Lord Jesus. This is the only place in the letter where the believers' personal love for Christ is made explicit (rather than their love for one another or divine love for them). We are therefore left with an encouragement and a challenge about our personal relationship with the Lord Jesus, in whom we have every spiritual blessing and without whom we could not be a part of the church.

Listening to the text

(21) Tychicus, the dear brother and faithful servant in the Lord, will tell you everything, so that you also may know how I am and what I am doing. (22) I am sending him to you for this very purpose, that you may know how we are, and that he may encourage you. (23) Peace to the brothers, and love with faith from God the Father and the Lord Jesus Christ. (24) Grace to all who love our Lord Jesus Christ with an undying love.

Tychicus (6:21-22)

Tychicus may well have been an Ephesian; he certainly came from the province of Asia, having been linked directly with Trophimus who was clearly identified as belonging to the city (Acts 20:4; 21:29). Tychicus may well have had special responsibility for the area (2 Tim. 4:12) and was almost certainly known to the Ephesians. But it is primarily his Christian credentials which qualify him as a suitable emissary. He is 'the beloved brother and faithful servant [minister] in the Lord.' As such his responsibility is not only to bring news of Paul but also to encourage the Christians in their walk with the Lord.

In that sense, Paul is modelling in his own concern about what he has been teaching in the letter. Relationships within God's new community should be marked by a love and concern for others and a desire for growth (eg. 4:16; 4:29). Here we see Paul sending a special envoy, a fellow minister, to the Ephesians for that very reason. In a letter which lacks the usual personal greetings (perhaps because it was written with more than one church group in mind) the arrival of a personal friend and colleague would have demonstrated the level of Paul's personal concern for those to whom he was writing.

These two verses have 32 words in common with the equivalent section of the letter to the Colossians (Col. 4:7), suggesting that Tychicus may well have taken the two letters at the same time, the common or copied wording making sense in such a situation. Colosse was also in Asia, further east and in-land from the sea port of Ephesus. It would certainly have made sense for him to visit both churches on the same journey and might also explain the 'you also' in verse 21. His concern for the Colossians and also for the Ephesians is that they might know how he is and that they might be encouraged.

Final summary (6:23-24)

Back in 1:2 Paul opened with the same couplet of grace and peace, but this time it is reversed and we have the benefit of the rest of the letter to shape our understanding of what these terms means and therefore what Paul is saying. 'No two words could summarise the message of the letter more succinctly. For peace in the sense of reconciliation with God and one another is the great achievement of Jesus Christ and grace is the reason why and the means by which he did it.'[1]

'Peace' has been a major theme throughout the letter. Those who were alienated from God and from one another now have peace with God and in the new set of relationships that constitute the church (2:14-18). That peace has been achieved through the cross of Jesus Christ and made known

1   Stott, *Ephesians*, p. 291.

through the proclamation of the gospel (6:15). Now a new people has been created, marked by peace (4:2-3). The love now evident in the church has been brought about by the gracious initiative of God and made ours through faith, hence 'love with faith from God the Father and the Lord Jesus Christ'. Love is the inevitable outworking of the faith that unites us to Christ and makes us alive in him, just as has already been seen in the lives of the Ephesians (1:15). It is perhaps for this reason that Paul consciously selects the words 'brothers' rather than the 'you', which elsewhere has been employed to differentiate Jew from Gentile. He may well have wanted to emphasise that we have been made into a new people – no longer Jew and Gentile but one new man, united in Christ.

'Grace' also has run as an essential theme throughout Paul's letter. God's glorious, free grace makes us into his people (1:6-7). It rescues us and raises us with Christ (2:5-6) so that one day, like pictures in a gallery, the church will become a visual display of his unmerited kindness (2:7). Not only that, but grace is poured out on the church in order that we may have what is necessary to become what we are and love as God's people (4:7). Such grace is free and undeserved, enabling us to become part of the church, grow as the church and be seen as the church throughout all eternity.

Is it not that grace is conditional or exclusive; rather, it is experienced by those in relationship with the Lord Jesus, those who love him. Throughout the letter we have seen much of Christ's love for his people (3:19; 5:2, 25), of God's love for the believer (2:4), of the believers' love for one another (1:4, 15; 4:2), of the love a husband must have for his wife (5:25) and of 'love' which may cover all these relationships (3:17; 4:15-16; 5:2); but here we see for the first time the love of the believer for the Lord Jesus Christ. Paul chooses to end his letter with a reminder that although faith relates to the creation of the new people of God, it is also personal. We are saved individually to be part of his people. A manifestation of the grace that rescued us and raised us with Christ will be that we love him.

The nature of this love is that it is 'undying,' a word which may cause us some difficulty not least because it is difficult to know both how best to translate it and also to what it refers. The word is most accurately translated 'in incorruptibilty' and is often used of resurrection life (e.g. 1 Cor. 15:42) and may therefore indicate that the love which we have for the Lord Jesus is a love which transcends this mortal life and goes through the resurrection life which will one day be ours in Christ. In that sense it would fit well with the great themes of the letter and the glorious future of the church. However, it is possible that the word should be associated not with our love but with God's grace – grace which therefore extends through to eternity.

In one sense it is a false dichotomy. God's grace, which brings about the new community which loves him and one another, is what will be seen in eternity (2:7). Perhaps Paul deliberately chose a resurrection word in order to convey the eternal qualities of grace and the effect of grace on the people it creates. He may also have consciously included the article before 'grace' (not translated in the NIV) as if to say to his readers 'this is *the* grace of which I have been writing', thereby concluding his letter with the great theme so central to it.

These last two verses are in many ways a prayer in which Paul picks up the 'great qualities of the Christian life ... and prays that his readers may possess them.'[2]

---

2   Foulkes, *Ephesians*, p. 186.

From text to teaching

These final few words fall naturally into two sections, the first speaking about Tychicus and the second about the grace and peace directed towards believers. Both short sections pick up the themes of the letter, in our 'horizontal' relationship one with another and our 'vertical' relationship with God our heavenly Father and the Lord Jesus Christ. In preaching these verses it may be helpful to keep those two aspects of Ephesians uppermost in our minds but also to remember that in small but significant ways these verses contribute further to our understanding of what it means to be a people shaped by peace and grace.

Introduction

The very personal nature of these words should steer us towards an introduction which prepares us for the practical challenge and application they contain. Here Paul is demonstrating his own obedience to the words he has written in sending his friend and colleague to the Ephesian church. In the same way we cannot tackle these words without recognising the practical implication of what it means to have a concern for one another and perhaps, too, for other churches.

We might, therefore, introduce the sermon by contrasting Paul's writing to most Christian writing. As I write I have the people I pastor in mind, but I do not know most of those who will be reading these words. It would be all too easy for me in my attempt to unpack Paul's words to remain disconnected with those who read them. Not so the great apostle; his writing concern is now manifest in practical action. That comparison alone might be sufficient to challenge how we view what we hear Sunday by Sunday or what we read, learn or study in our private devotions. If it does not issue in the encouragement and growth of God's people, we have missed the point.

Likewise, we may decide to introduce the sermon by asking how we might know if the words of the letter have been heeded. What would we look for? What would we expect? Clearly there should be a marked difference in our attitude one to another, as demonstrated by the apostle. An introduction which raises the question of our response could then be revisited in the conclusion and would provide a helpful opening to get us into the text.

Conclusion

The precise nature of our conclusion will depend in part on how we choose to introduce the sermon. But it is important that we ground the text not only in the rest of the letter but in the very real expectation that comes from these words. Both sections should result in us doing something – in modelling the concern of Paul and Tychicus and in the outworking of peace and grace which is evident in the final two verses. These are more than theological truths; rightly understood, the great trio of faith and grace and peace will issue in a tangible expression of love, both for the Lord Jesus and for one another. As this is the only place in the letter where our love for Jesus is made explicit, so our preaching must also make it very clear.

Preaching outline – an example

1. 6:21-22   Live a life of love

2. 6:23-24   Just as Christ loved us

These titles contain the familiar words of 5:2 which seem a fitting end to a letter concerned about the life and love of the church, all of which stem from the love of God shown in the Lord Jesus Christ. But although they may serve as suitable titles, we must be careful not simply to preach the doctrines of the letter, but rather their particular nuances within this final section, which is both personal and full of expectation of what will result from having understood the letter.

Questions for home groups/study groups

It is unlikely that a home group will spend a whole session looking at these four verses, but they may be used as fitting conclusion to a series of studies, in which case the content of the passage and its connection with the rest of the letter is well worth the time spent in preparation.

1. Who was Tychicus? (Acts 20:4; 2 Tim. 4:12; Col. 4:7) What was so special about him?

2. What was he expected to do? How does this demonstrate the practical outworking of the teaching in the letter? What verses might help us to see this?

3. What is significant about 'peace to the brothers'?

4. Why should love be associated with faith?

5. Explain what is 'Ephesian' about verses 23 and 24.

6. Verse 24 contains the first reference in the letter to the love of Christians *for* the Lord Jesus Christ. What generates this love? In what way have you experienced it?

7. The 'undying' of verse 24 is probably associated with the grace at the beginning of the verse. What do we know about grace and in what sense is it undying?

8. How will you change in the light of this letter?

FURTHER READING

It can be rather bewildering to enter the world of commentaries on Paul's letter to the Ephesians, especially when the choice and level available is almost inexhaustible. It is always important to read the Biblical text thoroughly before turning to a commentary in order than we might grow in confidence in dealing with the text as we have it. The commentary should serve to make us clearer as we wrestle with the text rather than providing a pre-packaged 'answer' as to what the text means. Whilst it is very tempting to resort to a commentary early in our preparation, it will not serve us well in the long term and will not make us better preachers and teachers.

When using a commentary it is worth reading the introduction before turning to the passage in question. In doing so you will gain much insight as to where the commentator is coming from and what theological presuppositions he might have. Commentaries should, first and foremost, make the text clearer to us in order that we might be better at making it clear to others. Good commentators will interact both with the text and with other scholars which may then open up avenues of exploration if time and interest permits. Generally speaking, I try to use one or two major commentaries in my preparation, supplemented by shorter, more accessible publications, preferably written by those who are pastoring local congregations.

In his New Testament Commentary Survey, D.A. Carson describes Peter O'Brien's *Ephesians* (Nottingham, UK: Apollos, 1999) as 'The Best English-speaking commentary on Ephesians.'[1] I found it extremely helpful in many areas and would certainly recommend it as the backbone to a preacher's library. Harold Hoehner's *Ephesians – An Exegetical Commentary* (Grand Rapids, USA: Baker Academic, 2002) is also worth consulting. It is thorough, comprehensive and accessible. F. F. Bruce's commentary, *New International Commentary on the New Testament: Colossians, Philemon and Ephesians* (Grand Rapids, USA: Eerdmans, 1984) is good but does not feel as dynamic or thorough as O'Brien. Some helpful thoughts were also gleaned from:

+ Ernest Best *Ephesians* (Sheffield, UK: JSOT Press 1993)

+ Ernest Best *Essays on Ephesians* (Edinburgh, UK: T&T Clark, 1997)

+ Ernest Best *A critical and exegetical commentary on Ephesians* (Edinburgh, UK: T&T Clark, 1998)

+ John Muddiman *The Epistle to the Ephesians* (Peabody, USA: Hendrickson, 2001)

---

1   D.A. Carson, *The New Testament Commentary Survey 5th Edition* (Nottingham, UK: IVP, 2002) p.93

◆   Rudolf Schnackenburg *The Epistle to the Ephesians* (Edinburgh, UK: T&T Clark, 1991)

However, with all these commentaries I would urge some caution. There is a reticence about accepting Pauline authorship and a reservation in places about the authority (or relevance) of the text.

If time permits it can be helpful to look at volumes by Lloyd-Jones[2] and Calvin[3], from which pastoral and practical gems can often be gleaned. John Stott's *The message of Ephesians* (Bible Speaks Today)(Nottingham, UK: IVP, 1991) is heart-warming and practical and seeks to engage both heart and mind as the text is methodically considered. Of the smaller commentaries Francis Foulkes *Ephesians: an introduction and commentary* (Tyndale New Testament series) (Nottingham, UK: IVP, 1989) is certainly worth consulting.

Inevitably most of us will be limited in our access to books and the ability to develop our own libraries. I think it is always helpful to read books written by pastors (hence Stott, Lloyd-Jones and Calvin), but if resources could only stretch to one slightly more technical commentary and one smaller publication, I would recommend O'Brien and Foulkes, to which I have returned again and again in my preaching and my writing.

---

2   Lloyd Jones' Ephesians series is based on sermons delivered at Westminster Chapel. The eight volumes are published by the Banner of Truth Trust (Edinburgh).

3   John Calvin, *Sermons on the Epistle to the Ephesians* (Edinburgh, UK: Banner of Truth Trust, 1973)

PT Resources

RESOURCES FOR PREACHERS AND BIBLE TEACHERS

PT Resources, a ministry of The Proclamation Trust, provides a range of multimedia resources for preachers and Bible teachers.

Teach the Bible Series (Christian Focus & PT Resources)
The Teaching the Bible Series, published jointly with *Christian Focus Publications*, is written by preachers, for preachers, and is specifically geared to the purpose of God's Word – its proclamation as living truth. Books in the series aim to help the reader move beyond simply understanding a text to communicating and applying it.

Current titles include: *Teaching 1 Peter, Teaching 1 Timothy, Teaching Acts, Teaching Amos, Teaching Ephesians, Teaching Isaiah, Teaching Matthew, Teaching Romans, and Teaching the Christian Hope.*

Forthcoming titles include: *Teaching Daniel, Teaching Mark, Teaching Numbers, Teaching Nehemiah and Teaching 1&2 Samuel.*

DVD Training

Preaching & Teaching the Old Testament:
 4 DVDs – Narrative, Prophecy, Poetry, Wisdom

Preaching & Teaching the New Testament
 3 DVDs – Gospels, Letters, Acts & Revelation

These training DVDs aim to give preachers and teachers confidence in handling the rich variety of God's Word. David Jackman has taught this material to generations of Cornhill students, and gives us step-by-step instructions on handling each genre of biblical literature.

He demonstrates principles that will guide us through the challenges of teaching and applying different parts of the Bible, for example:

- How does prophecy relate to the lives of its hearers – ancient and modern?
- How can you preach in a way that reflects the deep emotion of the psalms?

Both sets are suitable for preachers and for those teaching the Bible in a wide variety of contexts.

- Designed for **individual** and **group** study
- Interactive learning through many **worked examples** and **exercises**
- Flexible format ideal for **training courses**
- Optional **English subtitles** for second-language users
- Print as many **workbooks** as you need (PDF)

Audio
PT Resources has a large range of Mp3 downloads, nearly all of which are entirely free to download and use.

Preaching Instruction
This series aims to help the preacher or teacher understand, open up and teach individual books of the Bible by getting to grips with their central message and purpose.

Sermon Series
These sermons, examples of great preaching, not only demonstrate faithful biblical preaching but will also refresh and instruct the hearer.

Conferences
Recordings of our conferences include challenging topical addresses, discussion of preaching and ministry issues, and warm-hearted exposition that will challenge and inspire all those in ministry.

Other titles from
Christian Focus and PT Resources

Teaching 1 Peter
ISBN 978-1-84550-347-5

Teaching 1 Timothy
ISBN 978-1-84550-808-1

Teaching Acts
ISBN 978-1-84550-255-3

Teaching Amos
ISBN 978-1-84550-142-6

Teaching Ephesians
ISBN 978-1-84550-684-1

Teaching Isaiah
ISBN 978-1-84550-565-3

Teaching John
ISBN 978-1-85792-790-0

Teaching Matthew
ISBN 978-1-84550-480-9

Teaching Romans (volume 1)
ISBN 978-1-84550-455-7

Teaching Romans (volume 2)
ISBN 978-1-84550-456-4

Teaching the Christian Hope
ISBN 978-1-85792-518-0

ABOUT THE PROCLAMATION TRUST

We exist to promote church-based expository Bible ministry and especially to equip and encourage Biblical expository preachers because we recognise the primary role of preaching in God's sovereign purposes in the world through the local church.

Biblical (the message)
We believe the Bible is God's written Word and that, by the work of the Holy Spirit, as it is faithfully preached God's voice is truly heard.

Expository (the method)
Central to the preacher's task is correctly handling the Bible, seeking to discern the mind of the Spirit in the passage being expounded through prayerful study of the text in the light of its context in the biblical book and the Bible as a whole. This divine message must then be preached in dependence on the Holy Spirit to the minds, hearts and wills of the contemporary hearers.

Preachers (the messengers)
The public proclamation of God's Word by suitably gifted leaders is fundamental to a ministry that honours God, builds the church and reaches the world. God uses weak jars of clay in this task who need encouragement to persevere in their biblical convictions, ministry of God's Word and godly walk with Christ.

   We achieve this through:

+ PT Cornhill: a one year full-time or two-year part-time church based training course

+ PT Conferences: offering practical encouragement for Bible preachers, teachers and ministers' wives

+ PT Resources: including books, online resources, the PT blog (www.theproclaimer.org.uk) and podcasts

Christian Focus Publications
publishes books for all ages

Our mission statement –

STAYING FAITHFUL
In dependence upon God we seek to impact the world through literature faithful to His infallible Word, the Bible. Our aim is to ensure that the LORD Jesus Christ is presented as the only hope to obtain forgiveness of sin, live a useful life and look forward to heaven with Him.

REACHING OUT
Christ's last command requires us to reach out to our world with His gospel. We seek to help fulfil that by publishing books that point people towards Jesus and help them develop a Christ-like maturity. We aim to equip all levels of readers for life, work, ministry and mission.

Books in our adult range are published in three imprints.

Christian Focus contains popular works including biographies, commentaries, basic doctrine and Christian living. Our children's books are also published in this imprint.

Mentor focuses on books written at a level suitable for Bible College and seminary students, pastors and other serious readers. The imprint includes commentaries, doctrinal studies, examination of current issues and church history.

Christian Heritage contains classic writings from the past.

Christian Focus Publications Ltd,
Geanies House, Fearn, Ross-shire,
IV20 1TW, Scotland, United Kingdom
info@christianfocus.com
www.christianfocus.com